'There's only one book in the world I would read about getting into drama school and doing good auditions. It's this one. I would be nowhere without Andy Johnson, his unrivalled knowledge and guidance. There is no one better.'

Vanessa Kirby (*Great Expectations*, *Labyrinth*, *Three Sisters*, *Jupiter Ascending*)

'This book is accurate and beautifully concise. I wish Andy's written wisdom had been with me when I was applying to drama school.'

Freddie Fox (Guildhall School of Music and Drama, *The Judas Kiss*, *Hay Fever*, *The Mystery of Edwin Drood*)

'When I applied to drama school, I'd never auditioned for anything before, so the dos and don'ts would have been invaluable.'

Kimberley Nixon (Royal Welsh College of Music and Drama, *Fresh Meat*, *Cranford*, *Cherrybomb*, *Easy Virtue*)

'I often feel quite nervous for actors when I watch them auditioning. If they read this book, I won't have to be.'

Anya Reiss (playwright, *Spur of the Moment*, *The Acid Test*)

'If you are serious about getting into drama school then beg, steal or borrow a copy of this book and you will have every chance of succeeding.'

Gerry Tebbutt, Head of Three-Year Diploma course at PPA (Performance Preparation Academy)

Andy Johnson

Andy started his career as a stand-up comedian before going on to write, act and direct for the stage and screen. He was a writer and performer for the BBC's BAFTA award-winning *Short Change*, and has won a Fringe First and numerous other awards for his productions at the Edinburgh Festival Fringe.

He has worked at several drama and dance schools as a director and teacher. Distilled from years of experience as a coach and mentor, his system of preparing for auditions has helped over three hundred young actors to win places at the UK's top drama schools. Recently 21 of 22 students were offered places on acting courses, most of which were at RADA, LAMDA, Bristol Old Vic, Guildhall, Mountview and Drama Centre.

The Excellent
Audition Guide

Andy Johnson

NICK HERN BOOKS
London
www.nickhernbooks.co.uk

The Excellent Audition Guide
first published in Great Britain in 2013
by Nick Hern Books Limited,
The Glasshouse, 49a Goldhawk Road, London W12 8QP

Copyright © 2013 Andy Johnson
The extract on page 75 from *Jerusalem* by Jez Butterworth is
reproduced by permission. Copyright © 2009 by Jez Butterworth.
Published by Nick Hern Books.

Andy Johnson has asserted his right
to be identified as the author of this work

Designed and typeset by Nick Hern Books, London
Printed and bound in Great Britain by
Ashford Colour Press Ltd, Gosport, Hampshire

A CIP catalogue record for this book
is available from the British Library

ISBN 978 1 84842 297 1

MIX
Paper from
responsible sources
FSC
www.fsc.org   FSC® C011748

For Roger Vellacott
A mentor and inspiration to many

Contents

Part Three – Practical Practice

Part Four – The Auditions: Winning Ways and Knowledge

Introduction

Winning a place at drama school is difficult. Really difficult. Way more difficult than getting into Oxford or Cambridge – and Oxbridge offer many thousands of places. The competition is fierce!

My research reveals that, for a typical three-year acting course, some schools have over two thousand people chasing sixteen – yes, sixteen – places. A couple of institutions report that they accept *less* than one per cent of the candidates they see. There are tens of thousands of auditionees out there every year, chasing very few offers.

However you tally the figures, the odds are extremely slim, and stacked against most applicants. But you don't need to fall into the dreary catalogue of 'most applicants'.

To *get in*, you are going to have to *stand out*.

- You are going to need to be original, really creative, highly disciplined and totally positive.

- You will have to be calm, courageous, truthful and completely focused.

- You are going to have to know stuff and do stuff that 'most applicants' don't know and don't do.

Tall order? This book will show you exactly how to harness and tap in to all these winning ways.

You'll be strong, confident, brave, inventive and articulate.

These pages will arm you with all the essential weapons and the mental stamina for what might turn out to be a sustained campaign. You will know how to access that crucial 'edge' at your auditions and in your thinking, because of your preparation.

An audition is over in a flash. You only get one chance once you are in the room. Many people blow it because they are underprepared and unfocused. This means they make mistakes, in the audition room and in their own heads.

Your work and thinking will be enhanced at all times, especially when in front of the dreaded audition panel. You have to give a performance that is mature, engaging, 'watchable', believable and not inevitable or predictable. Your audition won't be full of the basic errors in taste and style that 'most applicants' will be committing. It will be tellingly different.

You will know what you are doing. You will be in control of your work and your thoughts.

The panel will be able to concentrate on you and only you. The auditioners won't experience your fear, anxiety or bad habits. Neither will they focus on 'inner voices', or the strange commentator that plagues the heads of so many applicants the instant they start their speech.

If you want to apply for drama-school training, this is what you will have to do:

Research schools, fill forms, write personal statements and CVs; spend money on applications, audition fees and travel; choose up to eight contrasting pieces, work on them, get better at acting, brush up technical and vocal skills, learn about Shakespearean verse; do auditions, interviews and then recalls.

This book will guide you through every step and give you a major edge.

Mantras

Your drama-school campaign will be all about courage, persistence and self-esteem.

Sticking to the following mantras will give you all of this – and more. They are the underlying philosophy of this book and they need to become a part of your mindset from now on. Some of the mantras are about positive thinking; others are for your work.

Although I shall return to these and other maxims time and time again, please visit these pages often throughout your auditions and during your rehearsal period. If you can embrace and ingrain the ideas below, you will be armed and protected throughout your preparation and for the auditions.

1. Mantras for your head

It's all good and nothing bad! No matter what your confidence levels are, or where you are or how you feel, always remember, 'It's all good and nothing bad!' This will help to keep you positive and confident. These are the two major weapons that you will need. You'll obviously have to be objective in your observations on what you are doing, but by remembering 'all good and nothing bad', you ensure that you don't beat yourself up or allow situations to overwhelm you and/or your work. Use this in all aspects of your life from now on. Get – and stay – positive.

Make fear your friend We all run on fear, every day. It's part of nature: Darwinian, if you like. There will be times when you are going to be afraid, nervous, worried, even feeling the tingly onset of panic. Embrace these instances and accept that you are nervous, but then use this force to help your focus, or to aid productive work, honestly and with confidence. If you make fear your friend, you can utilise the fear to gain an edge over those who are merely scared, especially during the actual audition and interview. If you are just scared, or only nervous – nothing can be done! So banish panic and get focus: be a Warrior, not a Worrier.

I am not here to get into drama school! I am just here to do my best work
Tell yourself, 'I am not here at the audition to be judged, or scared, or even to get into drama school; just to do my best, most focused, in-the-moment work.' That way, there is much less to think and worry about. Hold on to this notion throughout your campaign, from *now on* it's not about getting into drama school, it's about calmly doing everything you can to allow you to do your best work, every day. Think about all this as you prepare; it will make you stronger because you can then operate without fear and without judgement as to whether your efforts are any good or not. Let this idea spur your spirit to experiment in search of better performance – always.

You only get one shot So don't blow it! 'One shot' may sound a bit scary, but there's no need to be scared: it's all good and nothing bad because fear is your friend and, besides, you are only there to do your best work.

So on the day, you'll be free to take a second or so before starting your speeches to remind yourself of what it takes to do your best work and then go for it! But make sure you can accomplish everything you aim for. Get used to hitting the bullseye in one shot. Be ready to start well every time, because for a focused, connected and effective audition, you have to start your speech well.

Be you, be true It's all you can do. Be you in the interview, be you in the room; be you as you work, be you as you perform. These last two notions may sound odd, since you are planning on being other people in your monologues. However, the panel will also need to see a calm, focused 'you' within that character. This may be tricky to get your head around, but stick with the idea for now. They need to encounter 'you' when you talk to them too. This is who they are going to have to live and work with for three years. So don't forget to have fun.

These ideas will liberate you and your aim will be true, allowing you to be mentally strong and cool-headed enough to step up to the plate, ready to do your best work.

2. Mantras for working

It's all about the words The words are all you have. Your job is to deliver them with credibility and clarity. Explore them. Respect them. Let them affect you. You should not try to affect them.

Change is good You are doing a two-minute show here. Therefore, you have to employ range, depth and journey in terms of needs, moods and tone, in order to keep the panel engaged and interested. Keeping the panel in 'the zone' requires you to supply changes in pace, gear, mood, tone and even rhythm. Use change and use it often. Don't stay locked on to one thing, or on one level. Change is good.

Start well, end well Collect your thoughts as the actor before a rehearsal run of a speech, or when at an audition. Ask yourself what you are trying to achieve here.

- Focus on the physical and technical aspects of what you want to nail down, or to avoid. For example, you can tell yourself, 'Don't drop energy and intention towards the ends of your sentences.' You can embrace fear and tell yourself, 'One Shot!'

- Then start to connect to the character.

- Visualise where they are physically and the situation that she or he is in.

- Get into what they want and how badly they want it.

- Find what that urge to speak is. What drives their need to say something?

- Then you can start.

End 'in the moment' and stay there for a second. Don't disconnect too soon, as this also disconnects the onlooker. Linger in the after-burn. Good or bad, no matter how you think it went in the audition, do not make apologies in your stance, posture or even verbally. Some people have even been known to say, 'Sorry, that was sh*t.' Why do that? You never know what others may have seen, or what they may be thinking. They could have a more positive view of things and might have seen something to make them think: 'Hmmm, you know what? Let's see a bit of that again.' Your premature disconnection or wave of negativity may tilt them away from their first instinct. You do not want to leave them with any millimetre-sized shred of negativity in their heads. End well, for them and for you. End well also because you may have to do your next piece and you need to be in a positive, clean space, so that you can start well again. So end on a good note – whatever you think just happened. It's all good and nothing bad.

Try it many ways When you are working, don't start out by trying to polish or perfect a finished, final vision or interpretation of your speech. Explore everything in as many ways, and for as many reasons, as possible. This will make your journey *sooo* much more interesting. Experimenting with many ways of approaching and delivering your speeches will open them up and allow you to grow your skills and vision. Go anywhere and everywhere, but come from *somewhere*.

Note

You are going to see similar ideas, exercises and instructions at various stages from now on. Often things like 'Get to the end of the sentence' or 'Don't drop off' are repeated – and for very good reasons. The point of a mantra is that the content ingrains itself as you repeat it. Many of these ideas will pop up again in specific sections, such as 'On the Day' or 'In the Room'. In these instances, I have developed or changed them to suit the context.

There will be many things to remember, along with lots of dos and don'ts, exercises, tips and reminders. You may not 'get' or perfect all of them immediately. No matter, keep plugging away. Acting is a craft and there is much to learn. You just about get the idea of one aspect of the work and then will come more things. While you are attacking these, the grip you had on other skills will loosen. This is natural. Stay on the case. The good news is: the more you do, the better you get. But it all needs application and discipline – as does getting into drama school. If you persist, the golden prize can be yours. But don't forget to have fun along the way.

Thanks

Vanessa Kirby, Doug Quinn, Clive Wouters, Richard Jackson and Alison Winter.

PART ONE
The Application Process

Which Drama School?

- Find out what each school does.
- Find out how they work.
- Find out what they are looking for.
- Find out how their application process works.
- Discover what you want.

Research

Ideally, you want to study at the establishment that provides the kind of training you are looking for. But whatever your vision is, don't narrow your options. Find the sort of place where you feel you might flourish in terms of the working and social environments. All the various institutions have their own ways and individual merits. Naturally, people will have their favourites, but try not to be *too* singular about where you want to be. There is a sort of unspoken ratings list, where *everyone* has an opinion and where schools slide in and out of fashion. Personally, I'm currently very excited about what they do at the Royal Welsh College of Music and Drama. They are terribly good, friendly and really interested in people. But that's just me… The fact is, drama schools are *all* very good at doing what they do. Competition will be very stiff and it is extremely difficult to get into any of them.

Each school also has its own training ethos. Therefore, whilst they are aiming for similar goals, they all have subtle differences in the way they go about things. The only way to arm yourself with knowledge of all these elements is to do the research. It's also worth noting that all drama schools differ in their requirements for application, entry, audition and recall.

Researching the schools will inform and help to firm your ideas about why you want to train and what to concentrate on. The panel may well ask about these things at interview or even on their application forms. If the spadework has been done, you will be able to accommodate them with a knowledgeable and pithy response.

Where and how to find things out

- Get a prospectus.
- Use the internet.
- Visit the websites.
- Visit the schools on open days.
- Go to the shows.
- Talk to students: ask questions.

Phone, email or visit the places that interest you online, so that you can order a prospectus and get details of upcoming student performances or showcases. Go and see the shows. Talk to students – they won't bite. Maybe get along to the schools' open days in order to get a feel for the atmosphere and the work at each establishment. These are really useful and very important research experiences.

Visiting the schools is a great way to gain an edge for when you come to audition, because the building and its aura will be less alien and less daunting on the day.

The internet is the fastest and easiest way to start things off. You can see blogs, check out alumni and find out loads more. There are also plenty of independent forums and sites that will be of great use in helping you to gel your ideas and form your opinions.

How to Apply

You'll need the following for your application:

- **Application forms or online application account on the school site.**

- **Passport-style and/or digital photos** – full-length for certain places. Increasingly, applications are being made online, so raid your Facebook... Or maybe don't!

- **Contact details of your referee(s)** These are the people who are going to confirm things like your trainability, reliability, affability and your possibilities.

- **Payment** for the relevant amounts. To apply and/or pay online, you'll need access to a debit or credit card.

- **Your personal statement.**

- **An up-to-date CV** (optional).

What's the process?

As I said, each school will have a slightly different agenda, but generally it goes something like this.

If you are applying on paper:

- Contact the school for forms, or download and print them out.

- Once they are completed, hold on to them until you are ready to roll.

- When they receive your application, they will then contact you with info regarding the audition and pieces. You will also get a date or choice of dates.

- Pick a date and confirm that you can attend.

If you are applying electronically:

- Go to the school website, click 'apply online' and then select your course.

- Create your user account. You may need to make sure your email spam filters are set so as not to reject correspondence from the school.

- Take care to fill in the application pages as they ask you to.

- At some point in this procedure, the school may ask for a photo to be uploaded.

- *When you are ready*, submit the application.

- Usually, they prompt you to pay the audition fee as you submit.

- They will then contact you with an audition date or a choice of dates and more info.

The forms – your first point of contact

It's best to man/girl up and do the documentation early. Then it is in place, ready for sending off as soon you think you are good to go. Application forms are made available at slightly different times in the year, according to each institution's timings. Generally, they can be obtained around October.

The 'paperwork' is the first point of contact between you and your goal, so start off by making a good impression. If it's easy to read and looks orderly, then you are already making a positive impression in the mind of the reader. It's important, too, to make a copy of your completed forms before sending them. That way you can be aware of what was written, and remind yourself of things before your audition. The schools often ask questions based on what you put down on your application.

UCAS and CUKAS

Just in case you didn't know, UCAS is the central organisation through which applications are processed for entry into higher education. Drama schools affiliated to universities, such as Central School of Speech and Drama and The Drama Centre, are currently hooked into UCAS for the first part of their application processing. Conservatories such as: The Royal Welsh College of Music and Drama now use CUKAS, which is the conservatory version of UCAS.

If you are applying to a UCAS or CUKAS institution, there is a requirement to register and apply through these bodies. They will process and forward the application(s). After this, the school in question will contact you with the next stages – usually an audition date, more info and a request for the audition fee. Applications start in September and run through to the deadline date of January 15th. You can apply later than this through the 'late application system', but they cannot guarantee you will be successful at this time.

NB: do not send any forms or press 'submit' until you are ready!

This is really, really important, and it's also where so many people go so very, very wrong. Send nothing until you have chosen your pieces for audition and worked them.

When Do I Apply?

Simple. When you have chosen your speeches and done some decent work on them. But there are deadlines.

UCAS and CUKAS application deadlines are mentioned above.

Other schools range between the end of January and around about mid-March. Check online at each institution. Make a note. Don't forget.

Be ready Way, way too many people apply for drama school with only a minimum of preparation and, as a result, they are very quickly disappointed and out of the running.

After you send the forms off, it's possible that the audition date(s) can come back *at* you within a week or so. If you submit before you're ready, you will be seriously under-prepared, both mentally and with regard to your performance. If you are not properly prepared – you could blow them all.

It could take a good deal longer than anticipated, if you engage in a serious quest, to find the right pieces. To maximise your chances, you must be psychologically ready for battle, armed with strong, confident and worked-on speeches. This book will help you achieve all that. So get going on your monologues, as soon as! Now, in fact.

Is it a bad thing to apply late? I am often asked if late application jeopardises one's chances. All institutions are after the best people they can possibly get. Therefore, it would be plain daft for them to snap up the first candidates they see. They can't know what amazing talent could turn up later. I am reliably informed that there are places available throughout the audition season. That said, schools will urge you to apply early, and you might well want to – just have a think about things. What is going to work best for you?

That said, there is little room for complacency. Form-filling is tedious and writing a personal statement can be an onerous task, but nail these as soon as possible and the whole start-up 'stuff', form-thing and writing hoo-ha is done and dusted. You get more time and space to hunt down the perfect speech repertoire and then to explore your choices.

These kinds of things have a tendency to be self-postponing, even without your own procrastinations. If you are anything like the typical first-time applicant, this is usually how it will go:

Around August, maybe September, you will think about getting yourself together, to start getting it together... At this point you may feel the urge to take a break, put things off and do something else; to do something altogether more pressing for a while. Pretty soon, what with being busy cataloguing your collection of unpaired socks, then a bit sidetracked by Christmas shopping and stuffing turkeys, you'll be staring down both 'February barrels' of a serious lack of attention – with time running out!

The bravest course of action is to take a deep breath and attack the situation. Start the whole campaign with a positive thrust. Do this to prove to yourself that you are on the case and not doing anything by half-measures. Forge and strengthen your resolve, from the very start, in the furnace of your will. Start well!

You should do whatever suits your strategy. You may not want a lengthy process but if it's their first time around, I usually send people up for their first audition at the beginning of January, once they've done all the office work and they have at least started the ball rolling on speech preparation; usually they have been choosing and working, since September or earlier. They then continue to audition through the spring without any seemingly adverse effect on success rates.

Stagger the send-off The strategic submission of your applications is the most sensible and significant action you can take towards boosting the success and quality of your campaign. Meter the dispatch of the forms so that the audition dates s – p – r – e – a – d – o – u – t. Then you don't get all your auditions in the same week or so.

I hear many tragic tales of people who have ended up with three or four auditions on consecutive days! This is no good at all. There's no time to reflect, or even catch your breath. Use your planned time between dates to mull over, for example, how you really blew the interview by not fully listening to what was being asked – and slouching.

Check your availability This is quite a significant factor, since there could be holidays abroad, exam dates or other serious commitments that could prevent you from being available. If you know of these, you could put them on your application and you could save yourself a lot of time and hassle later.

What if I can't make the audition date that I'm offered? Stay calm and contact them, or email a nice note in which you apologise and state the reason for your absence. In all probability they will come back with an alternative time. But only do this if you truly cannot get there for big reasons. Don't think about changing things and messing them about because it's a mate's birthday, or you want to go to a weekender. Also, some won't let you change dates more than once.

Save your fave In the light of the sobering fact that most applicants are lucky to get an offer from *any* school, don't get narrow vision about who's 'the best'. It should be about the best school *for you*, anyway. But you might want to plan to get your least-hot destination first, so that the inevitable shock-of-the-first-audition is cushioned by the knowledge that it was not your absolute fave and top choice. You'll then have battle experience to take forward into the next encounter. You'll be smarter, leaner and meaner.

Take it slowly I feel that a slower, more deliberate campaign is the most effective, particularly so if this is a first attempt. This way, you make the space to reflect upon your progress and to change things (especially pieces) if necessary. To maximise your chances, you should have a few more than the bare minimum of required speeches up your sleeve – or in any other location. A friend of mine, who has a great deal of experience in this field, fervently believes in ten as that bare minimum. There are many reports of people who have not fully learned their speeches by the time they are called upon to audition. Or they stall mid-flow, because they don't know them well enough. Sometimes, if asked to do one of them differently, they dry or just about manage to stagger through – because they don't *truly* know them. Don't be like this. Get a schedule and a system together, approach things in a rational, calm manner. This could be one of the few times in your life when you can enjoy the advantage of being able to influence a small part of your destiny. Over the page is an audition/application timeline:

June/July	Research your schools. Read. Surf the net. Visit. Look for speeches
August	Read all your research and look through speeches – on the beach.
September	Start *some kind* of work on *some kind* of speech. Just so you can train.
October	Get the forms or register online. Make some speech choices and get going. Start sending forms, if you are ready. If not – wait!
November	Serious speech work. Think about when you can feasibly send that first form.
December	Don't go off-duty over Christmas – but chill out and have fun too.
January	Application deadlines approaching (UCAS/CUKAS 15th January). Review your speeches. Send the last of your forms through January and February for March deadlines.
February	Change speeches if you need to. It's no big deal.
March	Most schools have closed applications by 31st March.
April	Keep things lively, confident and fresh. Don't let your speeches go soggy! Don't get weary.
May	Most schools are well into recall stages. A few are still seeing first auditions.
June	Almost done. But if you are still going, KEEP IT GOING! Don't lose impetus or faith.

Photos

Usually, you will need a single, passport-sized shot. It's quite easy in these digital days to take a digital photo and then upload or print it yourself. There's also the good old photo booth.

Don't get caught up in a professional photo-shoot situation and, therefore, in spending lots of dosh unnecessarily. The admissions person and the panel just want to see what you look like and then remember you after the audition. So don't get crazy with lights, hair and make-up (and that includes the *girls*). Inspect, in detail, the list of things they ask you to send. Some institutions will want a full-length photo, especially for musical-theatre courses. If you're required to upload a digital photo to an online form, ensure that it is a decent but manageably sized JPEG.

Costs

Check out your costs. With travel and accommodation, they can easily mount up. Depending on how many applications you make, there could be significant expenditure. The audition fees alone can set you back up to £60 a pop and they are increasing every year. If you live outside London (some auditions do take place in several additional cities), there may be a need for accommodation. If recalled somewhere like Bristol Old Vic, you may be required to attend a weekend of classes and workshops.

An audition can easily take up whole a day of your time, or more. If you are travelling to another city, you should budget at the very least £100 per audition (including audition fee). This is cash that you'll need to earn or that someone has to provide. All the more reason to be prepared.

So, at the risk of dull repetition, let me repeat myself – dully:

- **Be prepared. Do your research.**

- **Have your speeches chosen and learned, and do some work on them before you send off the applications.**

- **Post your applications in a staggered pattern.**

- **Save your fave.**

- **Work out your costs.**

The Personal Statement

This will go onto your UCAS/CUKAS applications and, if required, it will be submitted with other applications.

Everyone seems to dread this bit and gets into a regular state over it. Selling yourself can seem false and awkward – this is why actors employ agents to do it for them. If you are feeling false while writing, it's because you are being false. Use the truth.

Personal statements are simple – really – but dead hard to write, because 'you' have to write about 'you', which becomes quite difficult. This is also why the perfectly simple exercise of expressing why you want to go to drama school and why you want to be an actor can turn into a nightmare of soggy sentences and generalised expressions, rapidly making all your determination and sincerity seem very insincere. For instance, here is an extract from an early and confused draft of a real personal statement:

For some people theatre is about being in front of thousands,
showing off and professing of the many talents that they possess.
Conversely, for me, theatre is my muse and my destiny, which I
can ruminate and deliberate on, thus making the most of every
theatrical experience I encounter.

While the sentiment may be admirable, the tone and wording undermine the statement and turn it into gibberish. Reading something like this, one gets the wrong impression of the writer. Bad start. Apart from it not making sense and sounding pompous, the writer seems to think he/she is an eighteenth-century poet. Just write, more or less, as you usually write or speak. There is no requirement to get into the mode of professional essayist or to treat it like an A-level assignment. Talk straight.

If you are on a second or subsequent application… you will have more experience of this task. Use the fact that you are coming back for more to your advantage. Use it as proof of your tenacity and determination. Resist any temptation to use the same statement as you did the previous year, since your newly evolved stance and your increased maturity may well change what you want to say. Anyway, with luck, your year will have been busy and eventful enough to warrant interesting new info.

You don't *have* to include the points that are coming up. They are for guidance only, to enable you to make *your own*, thoughtful and truthful statement.

What can you offer them?

Generally, this would include:

- An ability to take criticism.

- Objectivity and vision.

- Honesty and truth.

- Courage and determination.

- Energy and commitment.

- Time management and punctuality.

- Focus and stamina.

- Creativity and fun.

It is good to show that you are committed and serious, but without going over the top. Let them know that this is the only thing you want to do. They also want to see that you are a decent sort who can take the pressure and get on well as a member of a cast or community.

They will be wondering if you are a good, reliable, affable person to have around.

Dos and don'ts for writing your statement

Here are some pointers that will help to produce a succinct, punchy and credible personal statement, avoiding the usual clichés that others will be falling for.

Do...

Avoid 'weakened' words and sentences Seek to avoid phrases such as: '*It is my passion*', '*I have a passion for the stage*', '*my great desire*', '*I love to become my character.*' These sentiments may well be true for you, but many other people will be trotting out these and similar expressions. The idea is to convince the reader that you are committed, focused and determined to train, to grow and to learn. 'Passion' may seem a strong word, but it weakens if you use it thoughtlessly or untruthfully. Other overused words and phrases:

Thrive. Strive. Wish. Push myself. Challenge. Comfort zone. Character. Creating a character. Immerse myself [in a character]. Dream. [My] skills. Passionate. Escape. Desire. Greatly.

I'm not saying don't *ever* use these, it's just that so many people use them in personal-statement-land and, consequently, the words have become weakened.

Write well Make sure that what you have written makes sense. Keep sentences short and simple. Don't sound too rigid or formal. The most digestible personal statements are in an easy, relaxed style that conveys exactly what the writer wants to say. Keep things tight. Get someone else to read back to you what you have written, so that your clarity and style choices can be assessed.

Use spellcheck, but check what check gives you Care and attention to detail can only make the right impression. So double-check for sense and errors. For example:

> *I recognise that hardships come along with the career I want to peruse.*

> *I want to train as an actor because I love the change of starching myself.*

Know what you want to write about This could, if pertinent to what *you* think and feel, embrace:

- What this art means to you.

- What attracts you to the theatre.

- What theatre does for the wider public.

- Why you want to train as an actor.

- What you need to improve upon as a performer.

- What you have to offer.

- An awareness of how exacting drama school will be, with regard to work, energy, commitment, dedication and focus.

- Some sort of statement of your resolve and commitment.

- An awareness of how difficult and tough the career of an actor might be.

Take the ego out What does theatre do for you? Rather than what you like to do in the theatre. A good statement should be about you, but not *all* about *you*. So steer clear of comments that make your statement read as if it's all about your ego:

> *I love acting because I love the challenge of creating interesting characters. I am also the centre of attention and I love the applause and the adoration.*

Okay, that was a bit blunt, but you get the picture…

Ask questions If you ask yourself (and think about the answers to) the following questions, you will know what to write about in your statement. Considering these questions now will also inform your answers at the interview stage:

1. Why do I want to act?

The way to find your true response to this question is to react honestly to it. Go on! Just try right now to answer that question for yourself. Be clear. Be honest. Don't think about writing it for a potential reader; do it just for you at this point – but do it before reading the next paragraph. Then, later, have a crack at telling a real person why you want to act – without them laughing. This is a great kick-start for your statement.

2. What do I want from a drama school?

Presumably, you want to hone your vocal and physical potential while developing your creativity and imagination, in an environment populated by talented, dedicated people who will inspire and motivate you both mentally and physically. There are plenty of other reasons too.

3. What does theatre do for you?

As a performer and/or an audience member? Does it provoke, transport, comment, rant or rage? Does it attack, clarify, confuse, laugh at, weep for, parallel, diversify, or even scare?

Is it not part of an urge in all of us to get together and communicate? To watch things? To hear stuff? To share ideas? To experience the needs and actions of others? To take in information?

4. What's the job of the actor?

In this book, it is to speak the lines audibly and connectedly in your own voice, moving naturally, or being still. It is all about how you can serve the work and the words truthfully, believably and with some degree of taste. They are the interface between the writer and the audience. The job of the actor is very much about how the characters they play, make others on the stage understand what they *mean* and *want*. It is not so much about displaying what emotions your character might be feeling or, worse still, displaying.

Don't...

Waffle Be precise. Be concise. The person reading your statement will have read very many of them. Give them a break. The ideal personal statement does not waffle or use too many words. Don't replicate stuff that is already on your application forms and CV (if you have one). Stand out from the crowd with crisp economy and precision. Personally, I think that around fifteen to twenty succinct lines would do the trick. You don't need to write reams.

Repeat Watch out for repetition. It is really easy to repeat these kinds of words: *performer, acting, actor, experience, challenge, performer, shows, stage, drama school, work, greatly* and *passion*.

Repeat Did I just say that?

Be foolish If your opening statement reads something like: '*Ever since I was little, I have always been star-struck,*' or '*As far back as I can remember...*' '*When I was six...*' Worse still: '*TV presenters have always fascinated me.*' Or: '*I have always wanted to be in the movies.*' – then you are on the wrong track.

All schools want to read about someone who is interested in and articulate about theatre, someone who is talking seriously about training for and learning about the craft. They are not that turned on by candidates who are primarily motivated by fame or fortune. But they do want motivated performers.

Get overexcited Avoid excitable claims and foolish statements that don't really make sense:

> *The thought of not going to drama school is unthinkable.*

Think about it!

> *... can't think of anything more incredible than performing all day in front of an audience.*

What, as opposed to performing to no audience? And all day, too?

> *He not only performs but sings himself.*

He sings himself?

Embellish or expand the truth Telling porkies is likely to backfire at a later date, when the interviewers ask questions based on a CV or personal statement that was not strictly accurate and is now probably something you have forgotten all about. The truth holds power and integrity. These things are impressive. Give an honest account of who you are and what you want. The same applies when talking about your achievements and experiences. Tell the truth, don't s–t–r–e–t–c–h it!

Be cheesy A really good way of taking the parmesan out of your prose is to keep words simple and not florid or extravagant. Instead of:

'This is something that greatly enthrals me and I have always had a huge desire to make this dream come true,' or: *'This has been my greatest and most passionate goal in life…'* What about: *'This is what I really want to do with my life.'*

This last statement is precise, concise and cheeseless.

Something like:

> *The idea of studying in an area that I feel extremely passionate about gives me a massive sense of enthusiasm and is something I strive for with every fibre.*

– might be better as:

> *I believe that if you love something and are truly inspired by it, then you should work towards doing it – whatever that entails!*

Again, reread things or say them out loud, maybe to a mate. Are you real? Are you true?

Examples taken from real personal statements that kind of work:

> *'I think the theatre is a platform for the storytellers and the actors. At the theatre, we get to see the story come to life, with all the sound, music and lights to enhance it.'*

> *'People have often asked why anyone would ever want to go into the acting profession, because it is so random and difficult. I know exactly why I do. I love the idea of studying and understanding a text and often, another world culture or period in history.'*

> *'The notion that the theatre can comment on the world and its people is fantastic to me. I have always taken part in as many*

productions as possible and tried to see as much as I can. I have also attempted to gather as much experience as possible, to learn more about acting and how to tackle any style of performance. I hope to continue to learn more skills…'

'…this has also helped me to be able to get along well with a diversity of people and their methods. I believe that these qualities have aided me in performing and rehearsing shows, as they enable me to operate smoothly within a company and adapt to different ways of thinking and doing things.'

'If I was given the opportunity to study at drama school, I would commit myself entirely to the training. I am determined to offer hard work, an open mind and dedication to learning…'

'I have a terrible fear of performing. This is a true statement. But this has never stopped me from seeking the fear at every possible opportunity by being in shows as often as I can.

I think somehow that this must be a major urge behind wanting to perform in the first place – the fear and the adrenaline of being on stage.'

'…either way, theatre is a great way of looking at the world, especially through the minds of geniuses.'

'The kind of experience I am looking for is one where creativity and boldness will be instilled and encouraged, in a place where I can keep learning and experiencing.'

'Last year's auditions gave me a taste of possibility and I really think I am ready to take this on. I know there will be a price for all the things I want to achieve at drama school and in life, but I also know that nothing's free and that there is no easy ride.'

These work because they are truthful. So don't nick them, cos that won't be *your* truth – unless the statement really is true for you as well.

The CV

A CV is not totally essential, especially if your applications are online. But it can make a difference. A decent CV should contain personal details and history of your education and theatrical work, together with any employment and/or other learning experiences, such as workshops and classes. It should also be readable. When they hold your CV, the reader(s) will be holding *you* in their hands.

Don't bulk out your CV for the sake of it. Better to be concise but honest if there isn't much acting or work experience to put down here. If you have lots of experience, still be pithy. People will want to see all about you at a glance and probably on one sheet of paper. So make it simple for folks to warm to you; be easy to read, concise and clear. Cos that's what they like. Tiny points, but all adding to the overall impression you ought to put across.

Start with name and contact address, then date of birth and age, height, etc. Next, list your education details and qualifications. Just do the last two schools and set out the qualifications along a line, don't use up space by listing them down the page. Then give your performance experience. Start with the most recent and follow a format of: *Part. Production. Place. Director.* You don't need to say 'played the part of... at... directed by...', etc. Be easy on the eye.

Follow all this up with other skills you may have, plus workshops, courses and classes you have done. Finally, any other jobs or experiences you want to include. Here is a reasonable specimen of the kind of thing to aim for:

CURRICULUM VITAE

Name

Personal Details

Address _

Telephone _

Email _

DOB _

Height _

Schools/Education

Names of schools and dates attended

GCSEs
English Literature B, English Language A,
Physical Education A, Maths C, French C, Drama A,
Combined Science C, History A, Religious Studies B

AS Levels
Theatre Studies A, History B, English Literature A,
Philosophy C

Ongoing A-Level [*with results if you have them*]
Theatre Studies, History, English Literature

Performance Experience

2013 – Assistant Director. *Doctor Jekyll and Mr Hyde.*
Face Theatre Co. Dir. John Smith

2013 – The Inspector. *Mario the Magnificent Marionette.* Edinburgh Festival Fringe. Directed and adapted by John Smith

2012 – Alex. *A Clockwork Orange.* The Studio. Dir. John Smith

2012 – *Run Around Sue.* Music Concert. Lockwood Theatre. Music by John Smith

2012 – Big Macca. *We Will Rock You.* Bates Theatre. Dir. Sally Jones. Choreography Sally Jones

2011 – The Falling Man. *Secret for a Show.* Lockwood Theatre. Devised

2011 – Theseus. *A Midsummer Night's Dream.* Kingswood Theatre. Dir. John Smith

Other Skills

Guitar   Grade 4

Singing   Grade 5

Acting   Grade 4 Guildhall

Workshops (etc.)

Summer workshop at _ _ _ _ _ _ _ _

Dance and movement workshop with _ _ _ _ _ _ _ _

Mask weekend at _ _ _ _ _ _ _ _ with _ _ _ _ _ _ _ _

Other Work/Experience

2011 – Worked in a shoe shop (Saturday job la la la...)

Applying for the Second Time

The main thing I need to say at this point is: Just because it is your *second* time, don't *double* the deal. By which I mean don't get into: 'OMG, OMG, I didn't get in the first time. I have *got* to get in this time; otherwise I am crap, a failure – a nobody!' This kind of negative thinking will not get you where you want to be. This is focus wasted on panic and anxiety. Concentrate on how you can do your best work every day instead of 'I have to get into drama school *this* time!'

It's all about the work, not about getting in, not about you. Make the stakes exactly the same as you did the first time round. Have nothing to lose. Besides, now you know more, especially if, like many first-timers, you were *totally* unprepared for your first attempt. Knowledge empowers. You now know how and where you screwed up. You know what's going to happen, the kinds of people you'll meet and even where to go and how to get there ;)

If this isn't a first attempt, then you have three courses of action:

1. Go early Get stuck in early in the season. If you did quite well the year before, the people at the school may well remember you. If so, this could be an edge to work on. The experiences of the previous year will also be fresher in your mind.

2. Do half early, half later Although I've just advocated going early if you are on a second campaign, it is also a good idea to consider doing half of your auditions early and then save the rest for maybe after Christmas. Doing this could help you to reassess and/or adjust your approach or allow time to change pieces, if necessary.

3. Do it all slowly Take your time; get your auditions lined up with space between them.

New pieces

The advantages to choosing new pieces for a second campaign are obvious: you are using new ideas and fresh energy, plus you'll be on your toes. If you stick to your old choices, there is a risk of fatigue and complacency because you'll be presenting something you know well and have worked on a lot – to no discernible profit. If you hunt down and work on fresh, sizzlingly new stuff, you will spice up your work and impress the panel with the fact that you are truly a seeker of new experience. You are not trotting out old material but putting time, care and effort into looking elsewhere.

PART TWO
Preparation and Attitude

Choosing Your Speeches

Finding a strong, interesting and contrasting set of speeches that allows the actor to show a range of characters, moments and moods is a crucial step towards honing a major edge. It is essential to start the hunt early. Be exhaustive. Be relentless in the quest for something fresh, something that reads well and that suits you; something that you have a connection with or a feeling for. There is also much to be said for unearthing rare or new pieces that have not been overused. Get a further edge by avoiding audition-speech books, because this is where everyone else will be looking.

I'm afraid that, unless you get lucky, there is no short cut to discovering your perfect monologue. This trail requires a dedicated search, with lots of reading. Spend a day in a theatre bookshop and have a good old browse through. Theatres often have great bookshops attached. The National Theatre bookshop and the Royal Court's are packed with new writing. French's Theatre Bookshop in Fitzroy Street, London, has all the new plays as they are published. There's also a ton or two of older titles. They are awfully nice there and very helpful. They even supply chairs for you to chill in. Of course, there is always the internet too – if you want to be old-fashioned and unadventurous.

Here are some reflections from a successful candidate on the art of selecting speeches. She pretty much says it all.

> 'With your pieces, I would say have a big session before the beginning of the winter. Find ones that you LOVE and could bear

working on for months on end. For me, the best way of choosing my pieces, was to find ones with which I felt a connection. I also chose speeches where I found the characters extremely interesting. If you look for your monologues as early as possible, this gives you a huge advantage. It gives you more time to work on them and the hassle of choosing is done with.' Jess

Making a smart choice

Generally, if you just want to scrape by and do the bare minimum, you will be required to choose and prepare three pieces. If you are clever, you will have a few more in the pipeline or on the go. One will have to be modern, in most cases. Two (in most cases) will need to be classical and comprise a main speech and a 'back-up', which may be called for in the initial audition, though usually it comes into play at recalls. But it must be there, ready on request, at that first round.

By 'classical', schools mean Shakespeare, Marlowe, Webster, Tourneur, Jonson, Behn and the like. Some places now state that they don't want to see translations: this rules out foreign writers of the same era – though you can use them elsewhere. If you are applying to somewhere that has its own list of speeches, you will also need to select up to two from this list, which you should be wary of using elsewhere (see below). The definition of 'modern' for speeches will vary from school to school.

Is there a list? Certain drama schools require you to choose from a list that they publish. Check their prospectus and/or website for advance details. I'm not saying that you cannot then reuse 'list' speeches at other schools, but other panels may not want to see endless renditions of the same material. Many people will try to get by with a list speech as their back-up. That's why it is best to have up to four classical selections under your belt, and at least three modern. If you really like a list speech and it seems to fit, don't rule it out, but have an alternative – just in case.

First things first Does it engage? Does it read well? Is the story good? This is a primal point and one to pick up on immediately. Even though the subject matter may be of huge interest or significance, the whole thing is useless to you if it is not engaging to read and therefore to act and, subsequently, for the panel to watch. The panel people need to be engaged by the speech, as well as by you. Double-scan your selections for their intrinsic interest and engagement. Test this by reading them to someone else.

What does it do for you? Go for something that resonates with you. Something you feel an affinity for. Don't settle for less. Ideally, the speech should choose you.

Balance and journey Is it all on one level? On one plane? In one gear? In one colour? Is there a landscape? Sometimes an extract may not be so effective as an *audition* piece, even though it really works within the context of the play as a whole. It may just be too monotonous or relentless as a 'two-minute play'.

Train as you choose The idea is to train yourself and hone your skills as you explore your potential choices. Encountering many options and working with these will deepen your range and skills. There is the danger that you might not engage with the performance aspects of the work till quite late because it is taking a long time to dig out those perfect pieces and, therefore, you find yourself in a performance limbo. If you are agonising over decisions, then kick-start your training by getting stuck into *something*.

What about a non-Shakespeare classical? One or two places specify 'only Shakespeare' for the classical choice, so watch out! Study their letter/website. If the audition information doesn't specify, or they don't mind, have a think about auditioning with a non-Shakespeare classical selection. Not too many people do them and therefore the panel might not have seen these so often. Edge! This is always an advantage and sets you apart from the crowd. You are doing something different.

Recaps:

- Does the school want you to select from their list of speeches?
- Does the text engage the reader/listener?
- What does the material do for you?
- Is there a balance and a journey?
- Train as you choose.
- Have a look at some non-Shakespeare classical texts – the panel will see fewer of these.

Thoughts from another student:

'If you are struggling to find your speeches, do not panic! You will find them eventually. When you do discover them, get the plays and read them. But also start work on and learn your speeches straight away! You will then know them so well, when it eventually comes to auditions. Trust me, there are people, even at recalls, who are worrying about forgetting words! If you look for your speeches as soon as you can and don't put it off all the time, you have the bonus of being so prepared that you don't have to bother about things like this.' Ali

Dos and Don'ts when making a choice

Do...

Do the 'do not dos' Study the 'do not do' audition information for each school carefully. Verify the speeches and characters they *don't* want to see. Refer to the advice online or in the prospectus for the schools you like. If they have lists, they may include texts from work by writers such as: Steven Berkoff, Jim Cartwright, Alan

Bennett, Victoria Wood, Barrie Keeffe and Sarah Kane. The point about these extracts is not that they are poor theatre or necessarily badly written, but stylistically, they may not allow you to show your full potential. Or they have been overused. Edmund from *King Lear* seems to be a particular no-no, as are drunken characters and spirits or ghosts. Mad people should be avoided, too.

Be sure you have covered the needs of every school with your selections Make sure you know exactly what each of the schools requires of you for the audition. For example, they may want three pieces – one serious, one classical and one light-hearted. Others have varying stipulations as to what constitutes a modern piece. Some say post-1960s, others will consider 'modern' as starting from the mid-nineteenth century. So have a few moderns on the go. Many stipulate a maximum length for speeches. These vary from one-and-a-half minutes to three minutes. I'd go for something around one-and-three-quarter minutes to two minutes.

Choose a good few pieces – have repertoire 'The more the merrier' should be the measure of your intention. You won't then be winging it on the bare minimum – so many people do this and then flounder. Afford yourself the luxury of range and repertoire. You can only get so far with something that you find just isn't right in the end. Perhaps a drama school will suggest that you change or drop a speech after an audition with them. If you have a few irons in the fire, you don't have to go through the 'looking' process all over again.

Try to stay within your range of play Keep the part reasonably within your age and playing range. I think that generally within a ten-year span of your own age is okay. You can even go older if the other speech is very close to your own age. (This is only my opinion, though, and it might not be shared by everyone on the panel.)

The real trick is to select material that suits you and your personality. If you are slim, trim and slight, then Falstaff will not be the right part for you. If you are giggly and cheeky, then Lady Anne is not a good match. Give yourself *some* leeway, though.

Deal direct A situation in which one determined person directly engages with another can be a very effective choice, because in real life when we talk to someone, we change and our needs change as that person reacts – or fails to react. A gritty monologue in this vein gives you the opportunity to explore the reasons for this engagement and also what your character wants as the argument unfolds. A speech such as this might also be more engaging to watch because things change faster than when a character is locked into poignant (but perhaps unchanging) reminiscence or recounting of events.

Consider comedy Laughter is always good in tense situations and can make people warm to you. If comedy is your forte, this could be the way forward. It's a good plan to have at least one lighter or light-hearted speech on the go.

Read your selections to other people, or have them read to you Do this to get a bead on how they might play and how they sound. Get someone to read possible choices to you out loud, so that you can hear them objectively. If friends are also auditioning, then share the burden. Have a read-through get-together. Use each other, help each other.

Keep it different, keep it real – but not *too* extreme Smart and committed students won't just trawl a couple of well-thumbed audition compilations. They will be reading whole works and visiting shows in search of something fresh and different, something that other people might have missed.

So make the panel's perception of you into one of somebody prepared to go the extra mile. Every little helps. This is also why opting for a non-Shakespeare classical piece may be to your advantage. Panel people get weary of seeing the same old chestnuts roasting away before them. Maximise your chances!

Keep it simple By this I mean avoid stuff with too many layers, which could distract the watcher. For example, if your character is talking to someone about what another person has been telling them about someone else and what they said, then the audience has to fathom out all these layers. I mean, wasn't it difficult enough trying to work out that sentence? This is just too much work for your listener, in this short window of time.

Try to look for positive material I have a feeling that 'positive' may leave a better vibe in the room than torturous tales of rape, abuse, violence, pregnancy, infidelity, etc....

Ditch it Be prepared to drop something, even if you have loved it. There are times when material that took a while to select and that you thought was perfect, ceases to work for you. Sometimes the speech will just run out of steam. If it isn't right any more, or it doesn't fit the requirements – let it go.

Recaps:

- **Scrutinise the dates and criteria for modern pieces, because they vary at each school.**

- **Investigate speeches and characters that panels DON'T want to see.**

- **Study the requirements of each school carefully.**

- **Have a few (maybe seven or eight) speeches on the go.**

- **Choose at least one close to your own age and playing range.**

- **Deal direct.**

- **Read your selections to other people or have them read to you.**

- **Keep it real, but look for something different or rarely seen.**

- **Keep it simple.**

- **Look for positive material in at least one speech.**
- **Be prepared to ditch it.**

Don't...

Necessarily go for something that is merely dramatic or heroic Quite often there is greater potential in more low-key extracts, which may well have a quirky charm and, therefore, allow you a more subtle range of possibilities and changes. You must continue to look for a journey, both in the material and for the character. Keep your audience engrossed.

Do two pieces directly to the audience If you choose a soliloquy for your classical, ring the changes by making a contrast in staging – select something that involves talking to another character.

Cry Unless you are really, terribly, awfully sure you can make them work, be on guard against tears. I have seen plenty of pieces where the performance becomes purely about the actor crying or attempting to cry or, worse still, 'acting' crying. Apply this thought to anger and grief as well. At times like these, the delivery often becomes more about acting and not, finally, about the material or truth.

Get seduced – watch out for drama! Don't be seduced by über-tragic pieces: they are not necessarily the most exciting, or even inviting to the panel.

Be enticed by lots and lots of swearing Think twice about really excessive swearing. Don't rule it out entirely, just be judicious. You can bet that plenty of first-timers will be thrilled by the opportunity to fill the stage with expletives.

Go for the 'shouty' As with the two topics above, the panels see Shouty McShouty from Shoutington on a very regular basis. I'm not saying don't do it. Just be aware that the speech and your delivery should not be 'ALL ABOUT THE SHOUT!' **LOTS OF PEOPLE WILL BE SHOUTING AND BULGING THEIR NECK MUSCLES.** It all gets very loud – and boring.

No sex, please... Well, not entirely no sex. Material of a sexual nature is okay but there must be more to the speech than just flirting, pouting and posing – and that's just the boys. The panel will have seen buckets of this kind of stuff. (See 'Change is Good'.)

Personally, I wouldn't do any speeches about being on stage, at an audition or about acting either, but that's just me.

Recaps:

- **Don't do two pieces directly to the audience.**
- **No drunks or ghosts, spirits or fairies. Study the 'do not dos'.**
- **Don't be seduced by extracts which might seem highly dramatic but don't fully pay off.**
- **Watch the tears.**
- **Watch the shout.**
- **Don't get *too* sexy.**

Making a dynamic contrast

The reason that the schools ask you for contrasting pieces is so that you don't show the panel the same character-type, tone or mood twice. If there is no contrast, or only a weak one, they will not be able to see your range – because you won't be able to show it.

Simple, eh? But this is a very important aspect to get right, so that they can see as much of your range and flexibility as possible. They want people who can show numerous different and subtle facets to their acting. Choose texts that will allow you to convince them of these abilities in your performance or, at least, let them see that you have the potential to evince these qualities.

Is there a journey? By the end of the speech, is the character in a different emotional or psychological space to when they started?

Carefully compare the extracts that interest you Are the characters too similar? Ideally, you need different character-types who experience a range of situations and moments in each piece. It also helps if their journeys differ. All this will then allow for potential contrast in beats, rhythms and tempos within the writing and in your performance. A good contrast will allow your malleability as a performer and your understanding of the characters to flourish. You should then be able to show some layers in your performance. So you must pay as much attention to what *happens* in each piece as you do to the nature of each character, since there is much to be had from contrast of mood, atmosphere, pace, tone and action.

All on one level – or the same levels of mood, tension, pace, atmosphere? Pieces that have variance in these respects will get you to explore more depth and range in performance. That's what the auditioners want. Find texts with 'landscapes' and places to journey to. This will keep the story going whilst maintaining the attention of the panel. The more you can keep the focus and attention of the panel undivided and not wandering, the better it is for you. The greater the contrast of these levels in your pieces, the more room for manoeuvre you have in your playing, for change and range.

A character shouting doesn't always contrast with one who's whispering Think about this! A sad person paired with a happy one, or a modern character coupled with a classical one, don't necessarily make a contrast, especially if they are both *similar* people from *similar* walks of life, in *similar* moments. The same may be true if you merely couple two pieces, simply because one is tragic and one is comic. It's about the difference in the essence of the people you are looking to portray.

Contrast the back-up When selecting a back-up Shakespeare/ classical text, consider the contrast with what you already have for your main speeches.

> **Contrast recaps:**
>
> • **Carefully compare your potential selections.**
>
> • **Is there a journey for each of the characters? Are the journeys different?**
>
> • **Are they on one level or in one mood? Are these too similar across your selections?**
>
> • **Contrast the characters as well as the content.**
>
> • **Look for contrast in your back-up text(s).**

Accents and dialects

This is quite a tricky area. In general, it's best to avoid dialects or accents that are not your own, unless you are brilliant at them. If your natural accent is, say, American, or your intonation is Geordie, then by all means go for it. In fact, if you can find a speech that is penned in your regional dialect, so much the better. In their audition advice many schools actually say 'don't adopt accents and dialects if they are not your own'. Otherwise there is a distinct possibility that your delivery becomes all about acting these and very little else.

They want to hear *your* voice. Also, if you are not spot-on, you will distract the panel, who will be listening to possible wobbles in the accent and thus diverted from focusing on your mighty skills, maybe even getting mildly irritated. This you do not want.

It is, however, possible to make a speech written with an accent or in dialect work with your own intonation. By which I mean you can use American material, as long as it's not *too* American. You may need to change or cut a couple of words here and there, such as 'trash can', 'highway', etc. You could use Scottish writing without the Scottish accent. But if the accent/dialect is 'written in' very strongly, you'd have trouble making it work in RP (received pronunciation) – that is to say, typically English, non-regional speech. For example:

> *Awrite mate. I'm just awa' oot the hoose for a carry-oot and it's a braw bricht nicht.*

It wouldn't work in Stoke-on-Trent dialect either:

> *Cos't kick a bo agen a wo, 'ed it wi yer 'ed an bost eet?*

(Can you kick a ball against a wall, head it with your head and burst it?)

Or the Black Country:

> *An yer gorr any on it an yer?*

('Have you got any of it with you?')

To which the reply would be:

> *Now! An if I had gorr any, I oodn't give yow non.*

The bottom line is that the panel would like to hear your own voice, wherever you are from. But you can be slightly flexible. If your character is a working-class Londoner, it is possible to make him/her work in a Leicester twang, if that is your own accent. Or if you naturally speak with a posher accent, you can get away with softening or making it burr slightly for regional types, but not so much that the changes mask your own, natural voice.

Writing by people like David Mamet (America) or Conor McPherson (Ireland), contains very specific nuances, subtleties, rhythms and sounds that are intrinsic to that tongue or geographical area. These are extremely difficult to make work in any parlance other than theirs, unless it's also yours.

When seeking classical work, look for characters who could conceivably speak the way you do, but cut yourself some slack. You could possibly argue that the Duke of Northumberland might have a slight regional twang, lilt or burr. Romeo's mates needn't all be posh. Don't stick so rigidly to the rules that you only have a tiny set of possibilities. The important thing is that you speak the words well, with precision and detail, whatever your accent or dialect. I worked on *Hamlet* with a young actor from Mexico who brought some really interesting qualities to the speech – and he got in!

Now you can start to think about submitting your forms That is to say, now that you have chosen, worked on, explored, decided against, changed, rejected and then done more work on your pieces. All being well, you can now appreciate why it is essential to start searching very early on in the game.

Preparing and Working On Your Monologues

'I find it hard rehearsing alone because I'm quite self-conscious. I haven't got anybody to comment or help me properly so I'm worried it's all a bit sh*t.' Georgina

Sort your head before you begin – make your rehearsals anxiety-free
Working alone can be… lonely, and scary. The following thoughts will help reduce excess anxiety and needless self-slaughter.

Have you ever done that thing where you are working with a speech or a part in a play and you've diligently done the research so that you have a really firm idea of the character? You've worked out in your head how they move and sound at every point in the speech. On paper, you've marked up the text with notes and beats and intentions and all that stuff. You have really strong ideas about the whole of the character and the ultimate soundtrack of how it should all sound, 'feel' and be at precise points in the speech.

Then, as you deliver your 'perfect speech', you begin to realise – what comes out is nowhere near all these ideas! What you have just presented sounded and felt nothing like your planned scenario was meant to sound and feel. Then you get a bit depressed, a bit like you can't act; a touch agitated and frustrated. Maybe you even want to cry a little, because now you fear that when you do the speech again, it will be even less like the lovely but concrete version that's in your head. Then you start to feel untalented, small and rubbish… alone?

Don't worry. Many people get into this situation. It makes them *not* want to practise. Every time they go to do work, they become fearful and have to drag themselves to it. Well, it doesn't have to be like this, because here is the big news: you do not have to get it right *immediately*.

Initial work on your speeches can be a daunting period in your journey. There is often no one to guide you or even to bounce off. It's hard to know just what to do with your monologue when you come to it for the first time. Just speak the words, introduce them to the world through you. Do this without fear or judgement for the first few times. Just go for it – whatever 'it' turns out to be.

Do not have a finished product before you start A lot of candidates for drama-school auditions will choose their piece, learn and then intellectualise the perfect performance, the 'perfect statue' of the character and the perfect way it should sound and feel. They will then try to recreate or work towards this finished thing in every session – without ever getting there. Because it cannot be done.

Acting is about process, journey and the exploration of possibilities. The longer the journey and the deeper the process, the better the possibilities will be on the day. You need to grow as a performer, alongside the growth and development of your character and of the speech as a whole. Find out what it is by finding out what it isn't.

So, abandon your expectations. Do not have a finished product in mind as you begin your journey. Take the anxiety out of the work. You don't have to perfect, form and polish a final product from the outset! In fact you must not.

You are allowed to be rubbish. So take a risk! Please allow yourself to take the risk of getting it wrong, being bad or failing while rehearsing, because you might be setting the bar way too high, way too soon. Take small, interesting steps; keep the bar low at the start. Fail, but fail well because you are trying things in many ways.

It can also be scary to work and rehearse all on your own, because it's just you – and 'the voices'. If you listen to the voices, you'll fall prey to doubt, fear and judgement. You'll worry about whether you or your acting are good enough. You'll wonder if you are getting it right. All this anxiety makes you squander energy by working too hard on the wrong things. You also waste focus by wondering instead of just doing it. Chill. Explore. Be a Warrior not a Worrier!

It's not about being 'gooood all the time'. When you are rehearsing and working your speeches, being *really* good is *really* not the point. Experimentation is the way forward. This process is about trying out ideas and exploring your extracts in different, sometimes extreme, ways. It is about exploration of the character, of the text and of you. This is what will give colour, richness and depth.

Your duty is to the work and to the words, not to being *good*. You're just an actor. Actors need to speak the words with clarity, conviction and intention, so that the audience can know and comprehend what is happening. If you are worried about being excellent or 'feeling' things, you'll never be believable and we, the audience, will suss you out – especially if you keep trying to 'do things' with the words.

Generally, when I watch audition pieces, people fall into one of two very broad, but crucial, categories: those who have done the journey and those who have not. And it's dead easy to tell them apart. I know who I'd want in my drama school… if I had one.

Persuading yourself to risk being bad can be a difficult notion – and spooky too. Risks can be hard enough to take when performing for others, but (with the wrong mindset) particularly so when working on your own, because you are often your harshest judge. So make fear your friend. Extend yourself and your boundaries. Otherwise the temptation to stick to familiar patterns and habits that are bad for you will be irresistible but hard to spot, because habits are strangely comforting.

It is through accepting the possibility of failure or not getting it right that you grant yourself the grace to take more risks and, as a result, improve. Then you gradually become 'good', because you have discovered what doesn't work – by doing it.

Of course, at the end of your rehearsal process you should aim for your best work and brilliance. A calm yet non-judgemental voyage will get you to your destination. A really beneficial by-product of this method of working is that you do not beat yourself up or feel negative when there's no requirement to do so. But retain your objective, critical faculties and then apply them at regular intervals on your way to said brilliance.

Let your destination become a part of the journey. Do your pieces with reasons, tasks or goals in mind, but if you have a fully thought-out end result in mind every time you do the speech, then you are setting yourself up *not* to get there. If you are judging everything all the time and then demonising your efforts, you cannot truly work, create and progress. Proper, objective, cool criticism – yes. But no self-slaying or negative vibes, please.

From crap you get fertiliser Don't be crap from lack of effort or low-energy input. Be not crap through dread and fear or lack of commitment. You will grow if you don't panic about being perfect all the time during the preparation of your speeches. The same applies to the exploration of possibilities: accept that some ideas will fail and some avenues will become culs-de-sac.

Kill the Demon... I believe this can ring true for many people, even seasoned actors. Often when you are working, a small Demon – a tiny you – will pop out and hover above you (or to the side in my case). It will sneer, snip and snicker while you are acting, saying things like:

> *You look really stupid with your arm out like that. How are you going to get that back down without anyone noticing? Eh?*

> *That sounded really silly.*

> *You didn't hit that bit right, did you?*

Or it will start to niggle away at the way you look or sound, or at what you are doing. While listening to the Demon, you'll be aware that a couple of lines have gone by and you were not in the zone. Then, while you are thinking, 'Damn, I haven't been connecting; I'm just saying these words', even more words or lines will have slipped past. Pretty soon, you're sinking into the sh*t. The Demon (who loves this whiff) is your harshest, most negative and least objective critic.

It is the smallest part of you. It will make you feel small and silly if you engage with it. The Demon is the source of 'the voices' I was talking about. If the Demon pops out, keep an imaginary pistol on you, ready to blast it. Or simply let it be. Let it talk – just don't listen. Do what you are doing. Why would you want to listen to the most negative part of you?

...but cultivate the Monitor Exorcise the judgement of the Demon when you are working. It will limit your creativity, courage, and shrink your soul. Naturally, you'll need to apply objective, critical thinking, but don't let the Demon beat you up. Stay positive.

Be aware of what you are doing, certainly, but let this observation be via a Friendly Monitor whom you love; someone who is cool, calm and serene. Let your Monitor be the kindly part of you; the one who can advise, and change things without self-punishment. There is a 'critical' difference between having an aware, alert, friendly monitor and *listening to* an ego-driven, soul-crushing, ever-talking Demon.

Get together with mates and form a group Have a gathering once a week in a decent space. Help each other. Use each other. This can be a powerful stride towards increasing your chances.

Here are some advantages of working together:

- Aim to meet from the beginning of your campaigns; you can then assist each other with form-filling and statement-writing. As I suggested earlier, mutual support while choosing and contrasting monologues is of great benefit.

- Share vital info, knowledge and experience. Watch each other at work, then give feedback and criticism. You will all be in the same boat.

- You can report and share specific experiences and audition nightmares at specific schools.

- Do mock interviews for each other. In a mock-interview situation, you can winkle out bad listeners and stubborn or misinformed, gibberish answers. All this shared experience will inform everyone of what *not* to do. It is surprisingly difficult to stand up even in front of those you know, let alone walk into a room, face a panel of strangers and say:

  Hello, my name is… and for my modern I'm doing… by… and my classical is… from…

  Or whatever…

  To do this in a calm yet alert way, without fluffing it, faking it, forgetting it or fidgeting – or any other 'f's – is not as easy as you might think. Many places won't require you to do it, but it's a good idea to get used to the experience of just saying 'hello' to the panel without feeling or sounding like a twit or overdoing it. Just to be open and up for it (but not doggie-keen) in front of strangers is a difficult and precarious trick in a tense situation, but one worth mastering.

- Observe people in similar or formal situations, or even at parties. Watch how they are when introduced to strangers. Check how they come into the room. Some folks giggle, others flirt. While some avoid eye contact, others seek safety by trying to stare you out. Sad types go all 'suit' on you and get your hand in a grip that could crush a Volkswagen. If you get together as a group, you will be able to tackle these difficult aspects of your audition with (and in front of) other people. (See: *'Hi, I'm Andy Johnson and I'm talented'* in 'The Interview' section.)

- You can also, crucially, take turns to be the panelists and see the whole thing from their point of view. You'll be able to identify really quickly what *not* to do and say. Shared mistakes and exposed bad habits will serve to feed and inform the others. They, in turn, will nourish you.

- Spot and mend people who wobble, wibble or dribble. These are the anxiety-driven tics, unintended movements or expressions that people exhibit while performing. There is more on these and how to cure them in 'Exercises Explained'.

- With regular sessions together, you'll all be in a position to exploit the above points and many more, while you help each other to prepare and work on speeches. The really powerful factor about getting together is that you learn as you watch, then share.

'My advice would be to perform your pieces in front of everyone, everywhere and whenever you can. You may not have many friends left to ask, but it will allow you to know that you can do your best, regardless of circumstance.' Annie

It is the preparation of your 'self' that will give you the edge I mention the word 'preparation' a lot. It's a word that may seem at odds with what many drama schools say about not wanting to see prepared performances at audition, and I completely agree. What they mean by this is a performance that has been prepared by you and/or a tutor to such a degree that it has no life or connection to the moment that the character is supposed to be in.

Audition panels often endure many speeches that are prepared by rote. The actor is doing the same thing that he/she always does, without any real spark or connection to the moment. They have practised and rehearsed the same old thing, in the same old way, and now the performance is tired and they are tired by it. In the worst cases, a set of worn-out, automatic movements and gestures accompany specific words and sentences.

When all the schools state that they are looking for potential in a student, they mean it. But the secret is to prepare your mind *and* your skills. You can be fear- and judgement-free, if you are prepared.

You, your character and the text can all be in the moment. You won't be trotting out knackered, empty moves and sounds that sort of *feel* okay but somehow, there's a little smidgen, somewhere, of something missing…

If you prepare yourself properly, you'll be electric, freeee and open, in a focused way, as if you had never said those words before and never felt those things before.

Go anywhere, but come from somewhere Naturally, though, you don't want to be totally random either. This is why I shall soon be reiterating maxims like: 'Change is good.' 'Try many ways.' 'Play/explore the opposite.' If you have been thorough, you will be strong in your head, strong in your character and strong in your decisions. You will be able to operate in the moment. Charged, yet calm.

Pre-work summary of ideas:

- Take the anxiety out of your rehearsals.
- Don't start out with a finished idea of the character – what they do, and how they feel – in your head.
- You are allowed to be rubbish, so take a risk – take several.
- From crap you get fertiliser.
- Kill the Demon…
- …but cultivate a Friendly Monitor.
- Form a group.
- Get an edge by properly preparing your mind and your material.

'When I started on my pieces I had simply not a clue about letting the words work for me, and truth. Looking back, this isn't necessarily a problem at this stage, if you listen and take the good advice!' Alice

Starting out – early thinking

Read the play, yes, but get physical with your pieces. *Simultaneously.*

Do some exercises on your speech as you read the play as a whole. This will get the words going into and through your mind and body. (See 'Exercises Explained' and 'Tackling your Speech'.)

The temptation will be to start 'acting' the pieces (and the words) as soon as you can. This is because you are keen to be a good actor, anxious to perfect your speeches and get them into shape as soon as possible – because they tower in front of you like giant locked gates. But don't seek this yet. If you unlock those gates slowly, if you use exercises and explore the words – you *will* be a better actor, and your monologues will find their own shape.

Form bonds and associations with the words. Conduct a physical relationship with them by doing physical things as you speak them, things like pacing out the words with your feet. Or even try clapping the syllables of the words with your hands instead of saying them.

Get them into your mouth, body and mind – as words. Not necessarily as the conveyors of the story or text at this point, but just as individual words. Explore them. Don't over-intellectualise too soon or you risk ending up with a performance that is not growing organically. Remember, you don't want a finished product before you have even started work.

Working on the play and your extract *together* will stop you from trying to see, hear and form the dreaded finished product, before the actor's journey of trial and error, exploration and experimentation has begun.

Just get the words out Whenever I'm seeing someone for the first time, whether they have a worked-on speech or are reading fresh from the page, I always say, 'Just get the words out. Don't worry about getting it right for now, let's just see what's there.'

Have a journey Have a steady, but thoroughly inquisitive, journey towards your audition performance. One on which you will have tried many ideas and have failed at many, too. In this manner, the character, the moment and the truth will all become something you can step into with familiar ease. They will be layers that you wear like a second skin. Make sure you are not rehearsing in such a way as to lock yourself onto one path and one way of doing things. Be really focused and in the moment, alive to whatever happens, as you work.

You are doing a two-minute play! Therefore bring the whole of the history and world of the play onto the stage with you. It's not just about the bit you are doing for your audition, in isolation. An entire universe of events, ideas and moments must happen in those two minutes – not to mention those changes of pace, gear, tone and mood – to invoke that all-important colour.

The panel will watch and listen with the same intensity as they would to a *whole play* of two hours or more, but distilled into two minutes! They will be super-focused. Everything needs to be condensed into an intense, rich, two minutes. If you have been doing the same even thing for a few lines, this could mean about a fifth of your 'show' has gone by without any change. Think about this.

Nobody wants to watch an entire play in which everything flatlines into one pervading mood or tone. This is why you are going to keep reading 'Change is good!' Keep the panel absorbed. Keep yourself interested. To bring the world of the play and its history onto the stage with your character, ask yourself these things:

- Who are you?

- Where are you?

- Where have you just come from or been?

- What happened to bring you here?

- What do you want? And how badly do you want it?

- Who are you talking to?

- Why are you talking to them? And what makes you start talking?

- What are you afraid of?

- How are all these things affecting your behaviour?

Work with these questions often. They will be of continuous use in supplying context.

Guess what? Change is good Change brings refreshment as you progress. Change will keep the audience immersed and interested. Don't be doing the same thing for more than a line or so. Your audience thrives on being taken to different places aurally (in terms of the patterns and sounds they are experiencing) and with regard to mood, pace and attack. These should all be subject to exciting and dynamic change, as the character's journey unfolds within the piece and as their needs and wants change within that journey.

If you were listening to a two-minute song or ballad, you wouldn't want to hear the same four notes repeated from start to finish. You'd get bored after ten seconds, then irritated; then you'd switch it off.

Don't be inevitable. If you have been going for it, then back off for a couple of seconds. If you are being low-key for a while, it gets exciting when you start to turn the gas up, then down again. Then maybe put the grill on, slap a slice of organic wholemeal under it, light the kettle, let it simmer, then cool, then boil, then – er, make tea.

Try the opposite, try many ways Explore the complete opposite of what the obvious or predominant mood and tone of the piece first appears to be. More often than not, this has surprising results. The 'opposite' can give light and air to a tragic or 'down' speech without losing meaning or punch. All too often, young actors tend to blanket their monologue with one overall mood. For a two-minute audition monologue, this is a mistake and will lead to unexciting, predictable work. If you go to the nub of things immediately, there is nowhere for you and nowhere for your panel to go. Game over.

Instead, why not provide a journey throughout the piece, for us and for you? If you have experimented along the path to your performance, there will be lots of colour and change going on. Avoid the obvious! At least for as long as you can.

Even experienced actors can fall into the trap of draping a speech with a one-mood mantle. You can prevent this by invoking improbability; right or wrong, good or bad. This will eventually nourish your final work. Delving into the opposite further diverts you from feeling the need to get it right or to be perfect while you work.

Look for the positive – even when the speech 'reads' heavy Be open to playing scenes as positively as you can, even if this seems contradictory to the text. Just try it! Also use hope in the same way. Sometimes playing hope or being upbeat in a tragic, serious, maybe tense situation works really well. It might inject an upbeat vibe into the onlooker. Despair can get tedious, especially if hordes of other applicants have decided to deliver despair on the day that you audition.

A monologue is a duologue waiting to happen Quite often, auditionees tend to make their *own* character the only focus of the monologue. Get used to including *the other person* in your thinking and ideas from these early stages. They – the other person – should be constantly involved. See the other person in your imagination. Place them there in front of you. Ascertain what effect you are having, or failing to have, on them. *See a face, don't just see space.*

Tiny (almost invisible) interactions and exchanges happen rapidly between us when we communicate. They take place as we think and as we speak. 'Other people' place constraints on us.

During certain scenarios in life, we become very angry, but we cannot afford to give full vent to that feeling, perhaps because the situation we are in will not allow it or we would not benefit from being angry. Perhaps because the person we are talking to would leave when we need them to stay.

We may be afraid, but if we show it, the other person would sense this and take advantage. We might be very upset, but if the other person sees this, she could feel sorry for us when we want her to experience something else. If we were to break down and cry, we would not be able to speak properly and so render the other person unable to understand us. Worse still, we might break down completely, and so never get the point across.

It is about what your character wants to achieve with the other person, not what you want to do with them emotionally. Besides, it is much more interesting to watch somebody trying *not* to be sad, or in love.

It is usually much more important that they *understand* you. Not that they see how you are feeling. Being clear and direct is way more effective than just being emotional.

Questions to ask in order to bring the other person into the scene:

- What do you need from them?

- What do you want to change in them or about them?

- What do you need them to hear or understand? How crucial is this?

- Are they listening to you?

- Are they about to interrupt you?

- Do you want them to speak?

- Are they failing to respond or to understand what you are saying?

- Are they in denial?

- Are they pretending to be bored?

- Are they getting angry? Guilty, sad or defeated?

- Should you press the argument or change tack?

There are plenty more questions that you can think up and employ to 'make it all about the other person'.

Make it your duty to tell the story As an actor, your primary task is to tell the story. Look to your character and what they say, not to the actor and emotion. You are only the actor; the actor is only the speaker. So tell the story clearly. Tell it with connection and engagement. Tell it with credibility. The job of the actor is to serve the writer and the words. Your duty is to the words and not to become caught up in displays of over-faced and unfocused emotion.

You are the prism and the mouthpiece through which the words will come. Engage the audience with the narrative rather than frolicking about on the stage. Get the story right and there will be very little need to 'act'.

Don't use tricks Acting is a con, a trick to get us to believe you. But you will not get anyone to believe you by using false emotion, strange voices, poses and odd speech patterns. The only weapons you have are you, the words and the truth – maybe courage and taste, and a few more… But more of that later.

PREPARATION AND ATTITUDE

Early thinking points:

- **Work on your speech as you work on the play. Get to know the words vocally and physically.**

- **Just get the words out.**

- **Have a journey.**

- Think of the monologue as a two-minute play. So bring the whole of the play onto the stage.

- Change brings refreshment to you and your audience.

- Look for the opposite. Try the speech many ways.

- Make some positives in your delivery.

- A monologue is a duologue waiting to happen. Make it about the other person. See a face not space.

- Ask questions about the other person.

- Make it your duty to tell the story.

- No tricks.

Note

Get on with it, get through it… But take your time!!

Put the brakes on… But keep the gas pedal down too.

Come off it, but stay in it. It is not about you. But then, be you, be true…

There are some apparently contradictory things coming up. You might read 'Let the words affect you, don't try to affect them.' Then you'll maybe see 'but now (for the point of the exercise) try the whole thing really angry, just to see what that's like'.

Bookwork

'You have to ask questions about the character to understand the character.' Sammi

Look at the book, work on the words! (See the next section: 'Tackling Your Speech'.)

Read the play There are no short cuts at this point, though plenty of people try to take them. Short cuts are a mistake – you'll get lost.

There will be no short cuts on offer during your training and probably not in your career. If at any point in your audition the panel should think you have not read the play, you will probably be discounted. Naturally, feel free to use study aids and the Internet to augment your efforts at this point, but only do this in conjunction with a proper study of the text as a whole.

Understand the story, the characters and, therefore, the context of your extract. Only then can you even begin to understand what your characters are saying and why. Also, the world and history of the character are then at your fingertips. Definitely *speak your extract out loud as soon as possible* and attack it with some of the suggestions coming up soon in 'Tackling Your Speech'. But bear in mind that true meaning and depth will only result from many facets of your work and research coming together in rehearsal.

Mining for facts and info Understanding a play, the people in it and what they do and say, is a matter of **mining** the text for **facts**. When there are no conclusive facts, then you need to **dig** for **clues**. If these are thin on the ground, then **pan** for **hints**. When the hints dry up, you will come to the point where you need to use the raw, naked power of your imagination to **plug** the **holes** that cannot be filled in any other way, in the constant search for flesh and bones for your character.

This work is paramount. Drama schools like people who can use their imagination to create the 'world' of the play and the 'world' of the character. There's a price on excellence, so:

Get a notebook! Make notes Many actors have at least one full book for each character they have played. Keeping a notebook will bring everything into perspective. The act of making notes gets the actor to think about things and allows ideas to form and gel. Here are some topics to make notes about:

Known knowns Find out what is given in the writing, i.e. that which is solid. What we know for sure. To steal a phrase: 'known knowns'. Write them down; think about them. This will inform you about your character and the story.

Known unknowns These are the things that are not specifically or directly referred to in the play. These are unknowns and you want to 'know' about them, because you have to *do* something about them. They are things that you might have to suppose and imagine into being, in order to make your characters live.

Ask questions – supply answers So, for example, to take a play everyone knows, if you were an actor researching the part of John Proctor or Abigail Williams in *The Crucible*, you'd get two pages. Stick down what you know on one and ask about what you don't know on the other.

John Proctor

Knowns:	*Unknowns (things to find out):*
• He's a hard-working farmer in his mid-thirties. • He has strong views. • He's not easily influenced. • He's married to Elizabeth. • He is respected and even feared by the other townsfolk. • He has an affair with Abigail – a servant.	• Why does he like control? • Why did he cheat on his wife? • Why is he attracted to Abigail?

Abigail Williams

Knowns:	Unknowns (things to find out):
• She is seventeen and a convincing liar.	• Why is she so precocious and manipulative?
• She worked as a servant on Proctor's farm.	• What effect might the violent murders have had on her?
• She got sacked by Proctor.	
• She witnessed her parents' murder.	• Why is she so determined and headstrong?
• She's the niece of the church leader.	• Why does she need an older man's love?
• She uses her sexuality for her own gain.	

When is this? Where is this? You should research the social and historical context of the work, too. What is the writer talking about? How can you, as the actor, channel the words and intentions of the writer? This is all essential spadework on the foundations of character and performance. Approach your extract as if you were preparing to do the whole play.

Salem, Mass. USA 1660s Witch Trails.

Written in 1952 to mirror anti-Communist fervour and McCarthy's 'Witch Hunts'.

Politics. Paranoia. Betrayal. Lies.

Based on real events. How people react under pressure. Moral fortitude. Flawed characters.

Who does what and why? Find facts about what happens and who does what. These will all build a complete picture, not just of your character and the speech.

Who says what – and try to think why

Abigail (or your character)

> • 'A wild girl may say wild things.'
> • 'I never sold myself. I'm a good girl. A proper girl.'
> • 'I have been hurt...'

Open your notebook so that there are two facing pages. On the first, write down everything **your character** says about **herself**.

Other Characters

On the other side, write things that **other people** say about **your character**.

> • 'She frightened all my strength away.'
> • 'Why, she's mad.' 'I wish she was.'
> • 'You'll be clapped in the stocks before you are twenty.'

On these pages, also sketch together the 'whys'. Thinking about why things are said will help you to find what people want. Fundamentally, it boils down to what your character wants at any given moment. If you start getting into *why* things are said, you will at least start to avoid wasting time on *how* they are said.

Population

Study the people of the play.

- What do they look like?

- Sound like?

- Smell like?

- How do they dress?

- How do they move?

- How does your character feel when speaking the names of others in the play?

The 'world' By which I mean the physical world of the character in the scene or situation, as well as the world of their head: what they want, how they feel, what they are like as human beings. Working out the physical world as well as the mental world of the character will add detail to the whole picture. You have facts and clues there in the writing. Bring your imagination to bear on what things look like, sound like, feel like and even smell like. Where is the scene or moment set? Conjure up rooms or exteriors. Create a really strong mental picture of these. Go into detail. Make it up if there are no clues. Envisage floors walls, carpets, curtains, period/style and objects that may be there.

As you start your audition, you will instantly be able to create this 'place' for the panel and for you. You will not just be in some room, in front of people… doing an audition speech. You'll be connecting to the particular place, time and situation of the character.

The panel will appreciate the opportunity to gauge your creativity and your imagination. So:

- Where are you?

- Is it night or day?

- What's the room like?

- Is it summer or winter?

- Are you hot or cold, hungry, etc.?

- What are you wearing?

Nearly all drama schools plainly state that they want to see you create and inhabit the world of the character you are playing. For me, this means the mental world and state, together with the physical surroundings. If you can imagine these into being, you will lift the energy, colour and sparkle of the piece, because you have somewhere to inhabit. This is also a key element in making a good start for your audition speech: connection and focus.

More questions

Why? The urge is often to ask 'how do I say this?' Never make it about that. Use your understanding, research and imagination to work out *why* the character speaks. The rest then starts to get real. If you do your groundwork on the page and use your notebook, you will be setting up reasons, questions and answers that will enable you to deal with the whys, the whos and the whats. In life, we speak because we have to.

What? Work out what the character wants, both in the sentence they are speaking, and generally through the play.

Who? If the words are directed at another character, then it has to be all about the other person, not about your character. Again:

- Who is your character talking to, and why?

- What does the other person look like? What are their physical features?

- What does your character want? How badly?

- What's the price/risk/cost of saying what you say?

Bookwork summary:

- Read the play.

- Mine the text for facts, information and things that will help you build the world and grow the character.

- Get a good notebook and make notes on what you discover and that which you need to discover.

- Who says what about whom?

- Who does what?

- Ask questions. Find the answers or invent them.

- Work out the wants and needs of the characters – especially your character.

- Ask more questions.

'Over the process I realised that acting is not about being clever or being this extravagant character. It is about seeking a real character by looking into the script and finding needs, finding wants, finding why they say and do what they do. I went in thinking acting is easy, great fun, you get to tit about on stage and be loud, and swearing was another attraction. It is still fun and I love it, but you have to do serious work as well.' Ben

Tackling your speech

It is disastrous to creativity if you 'set' the piece as you learn the lines! Form a relationship with the words – as words. Lots of people just can't help themselves. They *immediately* visualise the character, the piece and what it is all going to be, feel and sound like in their heads. Then they learn sounds and predetermined patterns that are very hard to break later on. Because, as the lines were learned, a bland tune of very few notes was composed. Everything that was 'stuck down' early in the work becomes tired and leaden.

Most people find it very difficult to shed the sounds they have laid down and the ideas that were plastered onto the speech, *in their heads*, when learning the lines. It will be hard to find spontaneity in your delivery if this is the case, because you will have become stuck in one worn-out way of speaking the text. They will also find it extremely tricky to change when directed to do so at an audition.

Encounter the words in ways that are wild and freeee! The work can then be open and in the moment. This will give you a passport to 'go anywhere but come from somewhere'! The 'somewhere' comes from exploring possibility, not from setting premeditated immutability into the speech at the onset.

Learn the lines by speaking the words, but not in an immutable pattern.

Understand the meaning Whether the words you are working on are modern or classical, you should absolutely understand everything written. Use a dictionary.

Find the rhythms Once more, don't impose *your* rhythm or too much drama too early, if at all. Instead, find out the writer's rhythm. Modern or classical, the punctuation in either genre will give up the rhythms to you if you explore and exploit it. So:

Find the punctuation The next bit of groundwork will be in determining the length of each thought or idea, each change of subject, so that you can mark out where the thought ends or changes. The punctuation will help to signpost and delineate thoughts, how they are changing, and show the speech patterns of the character. In a sec we'll look at how to work on punctuation, but for the moment just have a good look at the punctuation in the extract below. Take a much closer look than you usually do when reading text.

See how short the utterances are in this piece:

JOHNNY. It's all right, boy. Don't be scared. Here. Sit down. On that.

MARKY *sits on the drum.*

There. Now, there's something I'm gonna tell you. Your mum won't like this, so listen hard, because I'm only tellin' it once.

He lights a cigarette. Wipes his nose, shows MARKY.

See that. That's blood. And not just any blood. That's Byron blood. Now listen to me, now, and listen good, because this is important. (*Beat.*) I used to jump. Across Wiltshire, south-west. All over. One day here, ten thousand people showed up. In Stoyer's Field, half a mile from here, they lined up thirteen double-decker buses. Fair Day like today. But wet.

Raining. The ground was soft as butter. Stoyer's Field slopes left to right and it's rutted. On the day, the wind was blowing straight down the field. (*Pause.*) And I raced down the ramp.

And I took off. I hit that last bus so hard my boots came off.

Jez Butterworth, *Jerusalem*

Punctuation, especially in modern text, is often overlooked. The tendency is for it to become invisible, in much the same way as stage directions do to an impatient or careless eye. But there is sooo much to be gleaned from studying the marks left by the writer in order to meter, separate and highlight the flow of their (and the chararcter's) words.

Ellipses, or three dots (…) will often signify a disappearing thought or one tha… (…t has trailed off – like that one). Maybe something has been left out.

JOHNNY. What's your point, caller?

WESLEY. Nothing. What? Nothing. Just...

But why? Was the thought superseded by another, more important one? Was it too dangerous or too awful to iterate? You need to know or imagine what's missing.

The majority of students at audition do not pay enough (or any) attention to what their character was *about* to say or *failed* to say. Therefore, what they do actually say is not rooted. The student just falls into a relentless flow of sounds that are not truly connected to the character's thought patterns.

Punctuation can also help you to see how the character is speaking. Study the marks in *your* texts and see what is there for you, and for your character. They are gifted by the writer.

Commas will separate thoughts or bracket parts of it:

'The King, standing in front of the scaffold, said his prayers.'

Dashes may often indicate broken thought:

'I need a good, sharp, carving knife – not the serrated one, that's for bread – to carve this joint.'

New thoughts usually come after big punctuation (**.!?**) and will need a change of attack, fresh impetus or new energy. Now you have really looked at and thought about the punctuation, here are further ways to explore these marks.

Exercises to make a physical and an intellectual relationship with the words and punctuation in the text

Walk through the speech below (and then your own speeches), but do something physical with **every** punctuation point.

In the extract below, my marks are as follows:

/ = a change or separation within the thought: in other words **,** or **;** or **:**

// = end of a thought. Notice the end of a thought comes with major punctuation **!** or **.** or **?**

Your moves for the punctuation Let's say for separations (**/**), you take a step, back, forward or to the side (any is okay). Concentrate hard and only take the step *after* the punctuation and *before* saying the next word. Get used to being precise!

For the end of a thought (**//**), you turn left or right, or turn round, even. So:

O, **/** [*Step for separation*] yet, **/** [*Step*] for God's sake, **/**
[*Step*] go not to these wars! **//** [*Turn, because it is the end of the thought*]
The time was, **/** [*Step*] father, **/** [*Step*] that you broke your word, **/** [*Step*]
When you were more endeared to it than now; **/** [*Step*]
When your own Percy, **/** [*Step*] when my heart's dear Harry, **/** [*Step*]
Threw many a northward look to see his father
Bring up his powers; **/** [*Step*] but he did long in vain. **//**
[*Turn*]
Who then persuaded you to stay at home? **//** [*Turn*]

...And so on.

Apply this to your own speeches when you get them or if you have them already.

When you are looking at the speech on paper, you can also physicalise your response to words, groups of words and to the punctuation marks. This is also a great way to start your line-learning.

Exercises to find and physicalise the words in the text

Characters In your speech, every time you see mention of **characters** – these might be **people, animals, gods, spirits**, etc. – make a physical move, like a step or a click on that word. Really 'place' that word vocally, as you make the move or gesture.

Both actions should happen simultaneously. Don't drop the other words while you are at it.

Places Do the same for **places**. Such as **Heaven, world, globe, grave**, etc. Use a gesture or physicalisation different from the one you employed for characters.

Verbs and nouns You can also physicalise with **verbs** and with **nouns**.

The physical exercises below will acquaint you with the text without the need to 'act' or interpret too soon. At the same time you will be covering basic, but essential, groundwork on your speeches. All this will work for modern lines, too.

For now let's just deal with actions for the characters and the places.

Actions for the *characters* in the text When you come to a person or character in the text, take a *small jump*:

> O, yet, for **God's** [*Jump for person*] sake, go not to these wars!
> The time was, **father,** [*Jump*] that **you** [*Jump*] broke your word,

And so on…

Actions for places in the text For every word that invokes a place, *click your fingers*:

> **There** [*Click*] were two honours lost, yours and your son's.
> For yours, the God of **Heaven** [*Click*] brighten it!
> For his, it stuck upon him as the **sun** [*Click*]
> In the grey **vault** [*Click*] of **Heaven**; [*Click*] and by his light
> Did all the chivalry of **England** [*Click*] move…

When you get the hang of these tasks, transfer them to your own speeches.

When you have explored your own texts, move on to…

Put them all together! After having a go at each (punctuation, places and people) separately, put them all together. It may be a bit of a mind-meltdown, but persevere. Apply these to your own speeches as often as you can at the early stages of work on each text. This will sharpen your focus and concentration skills; it will get you multi-tasking and you will be forming bonds between you and the text. I suspect some may be looking at this thinking 'Tedious!' But it isn't, and it's well worth the effort.

> O,* **/** [*Step*] yet, **/** [*Step*] for **God's** [*Jump*] sake, **/** [*Step*] go not to these wars! **//** [*Turn*]
> The time was, **/** [*Step*] **father,** **/** [*Step, jump*] that **you** [*Jump*] broke your word, **/** [*Step*]
> When **you** [*Jump*] were more endeared to it than now; **/** [*Step*]
> When your own **Percy,** **/** [*Jump*] when my heart's dear **Harry,** **/** [*Step, jump*]
> Threw many a **northward** [*Click*] look to see his **father** [*Jump*]

* Some texts have a ! here, others nothing. Things can vary depending on the text you are using.

Bring up **his** [*Jump*] powers; **/** [*Step*] but **he** [*Jump*] did long in vain. **//** [*Turn*]
Who [*Jump*] then persuaded **you** [*Jump*] to stay at **home**? **//** [*Click, turn*]

Carry on for the rest. Notice how much the speech is about a comparison between 'you/yours' and 'him/his'.

There were two honours lost, **/** yours and your **son's**. **//**
For yours, **/** the **God** of **heaven** brighten it! **//**
For his, **/** it stuck upon **him** as the **sun**
In the grey **vault** of **Heaven**; **/** and by his light
Did all the **chivalry** of **England** move
To do brave acts: **/** **he** was indeed the glass
Wherein the noble **youth** did dress themselves: **/**
He had no legs, that practised not his gait; **/**

…And so on. There's more punctuation info, specifically for classical writing, in 'Dealing with Shakespeare'.

Go back to the *Jerusalem* extract and see if you can get all this working with that. Or have a go on your own modern speech. You may have to bend things slightly.

Speech marks:

- **Don't 'set' the performance as you learn the lines.**

- **Don't just make noise – connect.**

- **Understand the meaning.**

- **Find the thoughts.**

- **Find the rhythms.**

- **Make your exploration physical.**

The following tip could be one of the single, most crucially important factors about your attitude towards performing. It is, in my opinion, the foundation of all great and truthful work.

It's All About the Words

A great audition, and great performances in general, are not necessarily about your acting or your ability to 'do' emotion, or indeed, anything like that. It's about how you convey the words that the writer penned. You must deal in truth, connection and conviction. It is also about your process and journey with the words and what you do to form a relationship with and then connect to…The Words.

It is not about how *you* can affect *them*, but about how *they* affect *you* as they come out.

They are the starting point and the end product of everything you have been doing. You have to explore them, use them, feel them and love them. Don't waste them! That would be royally dumb. Work with the words! Give them meaning, colour and texture. Shakespeare used all his words as missiles of meaning for the audience. Words are tools for the actors. Arrows of action. Bullets of bravado… er, I'll stop there.

Be intellectually connected as well as physically (vocally) connected. Don't drop your mental attention to each word. Don't drop vocal attention. Attend to everything, always. This demands mental and physical stamina. There is a tendency only to see important, dramatic or sexy words – auditionees seem to go for those – but then to forget about the others. All the words are all-important.

If you attend to everything, you will connect to everything – and so will your auditioners! But building the stamina to stay on duty throughout the speech takes time, patience and exercise.

Verbalise the words. You can't 'vocalise' emotion If you can get to grips with this idea very quickly, you'll establish an early base for truth in your work. Naturally, you will want to 'feel' like you are acting (especially at these early stages) and this urge to 'do' something to the words will lead you to make 'noise' rather than articulate 'truth'. Never 'act' the words or try to vocalise emotion. It is not wise to demonstrate emotion noises (such as a tearful voice in your throat or an upset whine, or a scared whimpery sound) *in* your voice, by vocalising them. Don't make 'noise', make sense!

What I mean is that you cannot make it *sound* right. It has to *feel* right. The imposition of emotion constricts the work and then it becomes forced and false. To quote a friend: 'Emotion is boring. It is the argument that is interesting.' Vocalising emotion also indicates that you are not being you, not being true and not using your natural voice. Emotion is already there, in the words.

Arrive at the last word in the line, don't depart from it Use it as a landing pad for your intentions and vocal energy. Don't use the last word in the sentence as a launch pad for the next one.

Speak well! By this I mean that you can't mutter, mumble, slur or speak like you do with your mates. So, this means attending to consonants and staying connected to word endings, righ'? Sorry, I meant 'Right?' So many peopw don't observe 'll' and 'l' sounds, others faiw (fail) to pronounce consonants like 'p's and 't's. The result is that words lose energy and vibrancy. Even people with impediments in their speech can master these things.

If you're not speaking well in your audition, you lose clarity and 'zing'. You'll become dull and the panel will start to shut down. You should always be 'on voice', with vocal charge and the appropriate pressure and power within your speech, even when talking quietly or in a low key.

The major, vital, crucial thing to embrace here is the fact that you need to be able to speak well, in order to act well. That is to say, speak *properly*. Say 'string', not '*sh*tring'. Forgive me for stating the blatan*t* bu*t*... Theatre is, first and foremos*t*, a verba*l* communication. Auditions most certainly are. So you'*ll* need to be *able* (as opposed to '*abuww*') to be heard, understoo*d* an*d* no*t* sound du*ll* (as opposed to '*duww*'). In France, the audience is often referred to as '*les auditeurs*' – the listeners. Your ability to speak well is crucial, and the panel will be listening for this.

You don't need to go completely overboard, but you do need to attend to *fings* and *fink* about being *forough*. Lots of *peopuw feeuw uncomftubuw wiv* making the leap from *shtreet* to *shtage* for some reason. Don't be one of them! The next two sections will help to get you speaking well. Of course, I am not suggesting that you personally speak in the way I've just indicated – but many do.

Here it comes again *Speak* the words! Don't sing them. Say each word clearly, with proper diction and meaning. Do not impose your 'acting rhythms' on them either. (This is merely a place to hide.) If you don't connect to meaning and merely make 'acted' vocal patterns, then you are just making drama noises. So connect!

Love the consonant Consonants tell you where a word starts, what's in the middle and how it ends. Love and use the much-overlooked consonant. I'm probably preaching to the converted, but many people never even think about engaging with accura*te* diction. A lot of woul*d*-be actors don'*t* seem to wan*t* *to* spea*k* we*ll*, because it feels odd. Use your own voice, but speak the words with more care and attention than you would in everyday life. Words need to be connected, injected and not disrespected. They have to be individually energised, enjoyed and engaged. If you speak Shakespearean lines well, then half the work is done for you.

I don't mean that you should madly over-pronounce everything, but, for the exercise, have a go at really using the consonants here:

O, ye*t*, for God'*s* *s*ake, go no*t* *t*o these wars!
The time was, father, tha*t* you bro*k*e your wor*d*,

When you were more endeared to it than now;
When your own Percy, when my heart's dear Harry,
Threw many a northward look to see his father
Bring up his powers; but he did long in vain.
Who then persuaded you to stay at home?

Using consonants in your everyday communication will help give you clarity, power and authority on the stage.

Check out the sounds Upon inspection of words and their meaning, their rhythms, sounds and associations, a whole world seems to open up. Just connecting with the consonants will often unlock other doors for you. They will provide more clues, especially with classical texts, as to how the character was written and even highlight the way in which they are speaking at any given moment. Looking at that opening line again, we see that Lady Percy is talking with strength and persuasion. The 'T's, the 'S's and the 'O's are quite striking and they jump from the steady impact of all those single syllable words. Then there are the ways the sounds are used:

O, yet, for God's sake, go not to these wars!

All these are deliberate.

In fact, it is wise to assume that all writers have deliberately constructed the rhythms, sounds, associations and cadences in what they write. They will have worked and considered every word. Therefore you must do the same. It is no accident that Viola says in her *Twelfth Night* couplet:

O time! Thou must untangle this, not I;
It is too hard a knot for me t'untie!

The play between 'knot', 'not I' and 'untie', is a delicious reversal of sounds that winds us, in a physical tangle of words and sounds, into the 'tangle' of her thoughts. It also serves to entangle us into the ever-tangling plot.

Meanwhile, back at the castle with Lady Percy. In the first line again, look at the two groups of words that end and start with the same letter:

O, yet, for God's / sake, go not / to these wars!

If you really separate these you will get a hint as to how she is spelling her message out.

In the next bit of the speech below, what can you see, hear and feel from this if you really study and look? What are the sounds? Where do they interact or repeat? What about imagery and punning, e.g. 'Son' and 'sun'?

'There were two honours lost, yours and your **son's**.
For yours, the God of heaven **brighten** it!
For his, it st*u*ck *u*pon him as the s*u*n
In the **grey** vault of heaven; and by his **light**
Did all the chivalry of England move
To do brave acts: he was indeed the glass
Wherein the noble youth *d*id *d*ress thems*e*lves:
He h*a*d no legs th*a*t pr*a*ctis'd not his gait;
And **speaking** thick, which nature made his blemish,
Became the **accents** of the valiant;

The punctuation tells us that she is using quite long and complex sentences. She is trying to cram in as much as she can, to really get Northumberland, her father-in-law, to see her points and act upon them. To do what she 'wants'.

Last words:

- **Verbalise the words, don't vocalise emotion.**

- **Arrive at the last word.**

- **Speak the words and connect to meaning and intention. Don't just make noises that sound to you like you are acting.**

- **Love the consonant.**

- **Explore the sounds in the extract.**

'I started out with nothing – terrible diction, mumbling, shuffling about and loads of other problems and everything was very "acty". I had simply not a clue about letting the words work for me and also with truth.' Alex

Vital Edges

Positive actions to take while you are working

While you are working on your speeches, here are some things that will help to develop your performance skills and make for an interesting, balanced, tasteful, more exciting journey towards your audition, where, as a result, you'll be different and a cut above the herd. Don't forget, you are not just choosing a piece, learning it and perfecting it. You are now in training to advance your acting skills and intuition. And why not? You might as well improve and grow, even now, before drama-school training. Train as you go, so that you can achieve your goal.

Take out the ego And you take out the anxiousness. Try not to approach your speeches with the notion of 'What can *I* do here? How can *I* bring emotion to the words? How can *I* make them sound?' Work with the words from the base upwards and don't listen to your ego. By eliminating your ego you will get nearer to the truth and you will find it easier to stop 'acting'. You won't be trying to be constantly 'good'.

Chop it up Don't feel you have to work A-to-Z on the *whole* speech, every session. This can be daunting and less effective than sometimes chopping the text in half or into thirds, or into bite-sized chunks. Chopping it up makes for lighter work and allows you to focus on specific areas without all the time feeling the pressure of having to get to the end of the speech.

Explore the unexpected Keep the audience guessing; let them be surprised and drip-fed with new things that they didn't expect. Do this by being open to things that *you* didn't expect as you rehearse. By this I mean, don't keep doing the same safe things. Surprise yourself. Experiment. Even if you don't finally use what you do in these instances, it is good for you, and your speech. Don't know what's coming next in your speech.

Drop the safety zone; get out of your comfort space Look to unsettle yourself deliberately from time to time. Disrupt what you usually do. This can be invigoratingly liberating. If you are always comfortable, then you are probably doing something wrong. If you persist in doing the same thing every time you work the piece, eventually you will wear the words out. If you stay in a space where you are intellectually, vocally and physically comfortable all the time, then:

- Your work will be anodyne.

- You will not broaden your instincts and skills.

- You won't get any better.

- You will always turn out the same work and choose the same safe, comfortable things to do.

'Things' you think are good Embrace the notion of undoing the 'things' that you think are good in what you are doing. These are favourite spots that you get to in the speech, where you like what is happening and you kind of bask in them. These are places where you feel cosy. Invariably, these things you think are good turn out to be not so good. They are crutches and not the real deal. They will also become lifeless and automatic. They are just things you thought were good along the way. These 'things' may be:

- A fake sound in your voice.

- A particular run of lines.

- A move or posture.

- A shouting moment.

- A pause.

- Crying.

- A look.

- A list.

You will start to lean on them, and then they will become the only 'things' you do with the speech. These 'things' will become fake. Abandon what you are doing (if this becomes the case) and change! You will almost certainly have been playing them without spontaneity. You'll have been flying on autopilot. You won't have been in the moment. Consequently, you'll never allow the moment to change and, as you know, change is good.

Actor, beware the list! These extracts are from *Richard II*. Richard is a king pursued by his enemies and about to be overrun and probably killed. He comes to terms with the situation. Here are some lines from the speech starting 'No matter where...'

Let's talk of graves, of worms, and epitaphs...

Our lands, our lives and all are Bolingbroke's...

How some have been deposed; some slain in war,
Some haunted by the ghosts they have deposed;
Some poison'd by their wives: some sleeping kill'd...

Taste grief, need friends...

Before you read on, just think about what happened when you encountered those bits above. Then maybe read them again. Maybe out loud. When there is a list in a speech, you are likely to:

- Gloss.

- Generalise.

- Speed up.

- Build it.

- Chant.

- Sing.

- Get into meaningless rhythms.

- Act out 'hunting' for the words.

- Go off-duty or get sloppy and general.

...That was my list anyway.

A list is a trap that many just can't avoid. It's also a prime example of how the words and thoughts must affect you as they come out, not you them. Performers get a list and see it as an opportunity for 'acting', or they ignore it altogether, just spewing it out.

A list is a set of thoughts or images lining up in the character's head, not yours. You must allow the character not to know what is next in the queue, or even that there is a queue. Just let the list unfold. If you ignore the list, you will go to autopilot and cease to be specific. Then you merely churn out sounds that might 'sound' good, but signify nothing.

If they see the list as an acting opportunity, many people will go through a pantomime of demonstrating 'thinking-of' or 'finding-the-next-word'. Or they get into an auto-rhythm of sound as they reel off the constituent parts of the list, with no connection to the images or feelings that they throw up. Let the next item in the list affect you as it arrives. Then you can react and connect, within the instant. And don't take all day. A thought is generated at great speed.

'Let's talk' (*yes, let's*) 'of graves' (*they are deep and cold and in the ground and final*) 'of worms' (*we will rot down and be eaten*) 'and epitaphs' (*death-words carved into stone*).

> **Positive points:**
> - Take out the ego.
> - Chop the speech up. Work on sections.
> - Explore the unexpected.
> - Drop out of your comfort zone. Take some risks.
> - Reconsider 'things' you think are good.
> - Actor, beware the list!

Delivery tips

The following are ideas to stop you being boring in your preparation, then later in your audition. You can employ them to be more exciting and to get some vital variance of tone and mood within your delivery.

The One-Tone Trap – don't fall into it! We've been here before, but it's well worth a revisit because the One-Tone Trap is so common and such a speech-killer. Lots of people do their thing all on one level and with no variation in:

- Tone.

- Mood.

- Pace.

- Rhythm.

- General attack.

Two minutes, played out all in one tone and all at one pace, are two increasingly predictable and boring minutes – well before even one of which ends, the panel will the entering the 'zzz-zone'.

It's easy to fall into the trap if you are not wary or smart. As you prepare, ensure that there is variation in your delivery; keep the panel awake. Actually, do this to keep yourself engaged too. Avoid predictability.

Exercises To climb out of the trap, try the speech in different ways. Consider ridiculously impossible moods or character decisions. Go through the text in up to ten different ways per session. But these 'takes' on meaning, mood and character must be done full-on, from the first word to the last. Doing this will shake the pieces up and give you ideas. Often you will find something that, against all the odds, works. Perhaps your character laughs when they should be sad. Maybe they are positive and upbeat when the mood of the text suggests that they ought to be in a negative, angry state.

Or do the speech remorselessly in the most obvious and prominent tone. Take things to a monotone. You will quickly experience how relentless and boring it is to perform a whole speech on one level. You'll also discover how tedious it is to *listen to* something all in one tone. In one mood. On the same level.

Avoid complaining No matter how tragic the situation or how dire the straits, if you indulge in acting out tragedy, anger or any other single state mercilessly and for the whole speech, the panel will get snoozy on you. Your auditioners are not that interested in your demonstration of grief, depression or sadness.

Watch the whining If the mood is sad, tragic or downbeat, then relentless pursuit of these tones will lead you to sound as if you are complaining. If you persist with the complaint it will, in the ear of the audience, become a whinge, no matter how sad the piece. The whinge then becomes a whine. All the audience hears now is an irritating, high-pitched whistling sound, because you have lost them. If you still persist, they begin to lose any sympathy they might have had left. Then they start to dislike your character (and maybe you, too) before finally switching off. Game over!

Obviate the obvious Placing the character in a state where they need to cover their emotions is a really interesting choice to play. Give the speech a whirl without showing the emotion; think about riding over or hiding the feelings from whoever you are speaking to.

If the character you're playing gets very, very angry inside but doesn't show it, then tactically they may stand a better chance of getting what they want. If you open fire with the character at the peak of a mood, or even a 'want', then there is nowhere for them, or the audience, to go. Let emotions and moods rise and bubble on the inside while your character maintains apparent, external calm – until they absolutely have to blow. Even then, think twice about blowing.

Be aware of inevitability If you have decided on a run of words, a list (see 'Actor, beware the list!'), or swell of emotion or anger – good! But why not surprise everyone by *not* peaking? Divert, stop, shoot sideways, start laughing or slow down. This really keeps the onlooker engaged and on their toes, because what happens next will never be inevitable, either for you or for the panel. Often, a performance will follow an expected or imposed rhythm, flow or build. If the audience is subjected to a change in the middle of a build of something, then they get an unexpected treat. Take them where they didn't think you'd go. Take yourself where you didn't think you'd go.

Exercise to counter inevitability Go through your text but don't plot where you are going. Do not 'know' what is coming next. Deliberately surprise yourself. The outcome may be wrong (though it can often be sooo right), but it will open your performance out and allow you to access more in-the-moment potential. As a bonus, you won't be doing the same thing every time. Get into the moment. Be up for surprising yourself when you run a speech – but keep your clothes on...

- **Don't fall into the One-Tone Trap.**
- **Avoid complaining.**
- **Watch the whining.**
- **Obviate the obvious.**
- **Be aware of being inevitable.**

Note

I have been banging on about 'Don't impose stuff on the words, let the words affect you', and now I have just been talking about doing the speech many ways and in many moods. This, of course, is for the sake of the exercise, so that you can explore possibilities within the speech and break patterns that you may have fallen in to. This will also allow you to be open to spontaneity and connect to change in your performance. I have also been talking about you and your 'natural' voice, and now I am saying things like 'Speak differently from how you might normally speak,' and 'If it feels odd, it is probably right.' I am about to say 'use your voice' again. Also, 'Speak, don't sing!'

There is a balance to be struck here, so you need to use your judgement. Yes, you mustn't adulterate your voice so that it goes irritatingly high-pitched, or even too low, or underpowered. But you do have to break with your everyday speech rhythms and intonations, so that you have vocal authority, clarity and sparkle for the stage.

There are exercises in the coming pages. They are there to accompany some of the points I am making. I mention some of these in much more detail in the 'Exercises Explained' section.

Performance and delivery – honing your edges

The following 'sharpeners' are designed to hone your performance edges when you are in front of the panel, but it is vital to engage with these ideas right from the beginning of your rehearsal journey.

You want to offer a performance and an acting style that are mature, engaging, 'watchable' and believable, but never inevitable or predictable. What you do won't be tainted by the basic sins in technique and taste that many others will be committing. Getting things *right* on the day, by working consistently on these points, will make you stand out for the *right* reasons. So:

Stop acting This may seem a crazy thing to say to an actor, but I have been hinting at this notion frequently because it's an important one, but one that may take a while to get your head around. Get the basics right first – As an experiment, just say the words, tell the facts and strip away the rest. Certain schools might direct you to stop, strip it all back and just speak to them as if you mean it. Connect to the words.

Fix your focus as you start a speech In the actual audition, it is imperative that you focus before you start. The panelists usually say something like: 'In your own time.' And they mean it! But don't take all day.

Nerves, keenness, or the weight of the occasion will be tilting you towards a quick start. An awful lot of people do it. But now you know better. Don't just launch into your first piece and hope that everything will come together. It probably won't. First, tell yourself what you want to achieve. This will be something like:

- Settle yourself, you fool. Nerves are good.

- Make fear your friend.

- 'I'm not trying to get into drama school – I'm just here to do my best work!'

- Start well, end well.

- Monitor, don't listen and judge.

- Attend to every word.

- Don't drop off towards sentence endings.

- Don't wonder about the panel.

- It is all about the work.

Then, as you start to enter the world of the character, deal with the needs and wants of that character:

- Who am I?

- Where am I?

- Why am I here?

- What do I want? How badly?

- Where have I just been?

- Who am I talking to? Why?

- What do I fear?

All the W's. The more you get into doing this, the faster you can set it all up on the day.

Speak the words, don't 'sing' them 'Singing' takes place when you eelongaate the syllables or dou/ouble the vowel sounds. It happens because you experience the need to be doing something phonically or rhythmically, in order to feel like you are acting. Your job is to speak the words, to 'talk' them with conviction. Have a listen to yourself while standing with your back resting against a wall. (See 'The Wall' in 'Exercises Explained'). Don't move your head, hands or face, just speak. If the words don't sound normal, if they are elongated or you are 'singing' an odd rhythm, then something is wrong. You are possibly using your 'acting song' or your 'acting voice'. This is the voice, intonation or imposed rhythm that you think you need when acting. If you detect anything fake, get rid of it. This could take a bit of doing, so don't judge, or beat yourself up, just go back and fix it. Monitor in a helpful way.

People often use extended vowel noises because doing this 'sounds' more dramatic. It isn't. You are not really speaking the words. This fault is usually more prevalent in classical work. If you suffer from irritating-vowels and extra-syllables syndrome, these could be quite hard to diagnose because you are so cosy with and entranced by them, or even hiding behind them.

Exercises to minimise singing 'The Wall' or 'The Mirror' exercises set out in 'Exercises Explained' will help to isolate things, leaving just you and your voice. Try the speech, or a section of it, using very clipped vowels. Keep them short and tight. Really practise this.

Or, employ a loving or patient pal to write down all the elongated words they hear. Then go again with your friend making you go back and fix, if they hear any singing. The same suffering listener could also ensure that you are not getting nasal or high-pitched – not using *your* voice.

Keep the flow – don't be 'stoppy' This is a major problem and one I often encounter. Many people stop

at the end of every sentence or line.

Sometimes this is to gather thoughts –

...but mostly, it's to try to 'act out' the next bit of emotion –

The result is – that things are...

'bitty' –

    – scrappy and do

                not

                  flow.

Don't be 'stoppy'. You will slow things down and break the natural flow and vitality of the writing. Get on with it! Your speech should flow and pretty much keep going until the punctuation says: 'Stop!?.' If you're not saying anything, we can't hear anything.

Every time you stop, you drop the ball; you staunch the flow, fizzle the energy. As members of the audience, we drop with you. If you stop, there is nothing there for us to see or hear. This is especially so if you pause...

...without good cause.

Everything should be instant and happen on the line, or in the line. But don't rush either. Inhabit the moment but don't bleed it. Stay 'in' every word, just don't hang around, especially at the end of a line or sentence.

Some people stop because that's the inescapable rhythm with which they learned the speech. Some stop because they need time to gather or demonstrate the next bit of 'acting'. At other times they stop because they are trying to summon up the mood, in front of the line. Don't do this; make things instantaneous. Have the mood, have the tone while you speak. We, the audience, do not want to hang around with you while you dig up the emotion and all that other stuff, and then *demonstrate* it. The only thing we are interested in is what happens next. Keep the story moving, keep the flow, keep the energy moving and keep us moving!

Exercise to stop you being 'stoppy'

- **Fast** Train yourself not to stop by going through the speech very quickly, but never 'skim' over any of the words.

- **...But stay in it!** Also, go through the speech very slowly, so that you can get your head and vocal chords around each and every word. Then, when you do a fast run, you won't lose or drop any of them. Get on, but by staying in it. Just because you are going quickly, it shouldn't follow that the autopilot is flying. To avoid the autopilot, you need sharp focus. This takes effort, energy and perseverance. You should always be getting on with it but, paradoxically, taking your time. Gas pedal down but brakes on!

- **Beckon** Have someone beckon you on with the speech using hand movements. They must not let you stop or rest. They can even vocally impel you with something like: 'Come on, come on,' while you're doing it. If your habit is extremely bad, they could prod you. You are looking at the gaps, not the speed at which the words emerge. The words should always be owned and inhabited.

  If you are on your own, you could use an arm or hand movement to beckon yourself on. Keep impelling yourself. Your connection to the piece and to each word may suffer at this pace, but stay plugged-in, at least in vocal energy and intention. You might find that you forget the words at this point because you are out of the comfort zone and rhythms that you are used to.

There's more along these lines in 'Exercises Explained'.

Stand well Just stand straight with feet parallel and shoulder-width apart-ish. Be relaxed but not floppy. People tend to adopt 'stances' for their acting positions. This seems to make them feel good or, apparently, sum up the integral essence of the character. If these stances actually, truly represent the physicality of the character, then use them. But don't do random or unconnected generalised stances.

If you act with one foot slightly out in front and/or to the side, it means you are posturing, unless you have made a conscious and fully thought-out decision that this is how your character would stand. If you do the foot-out thing because it feels good, because this is how we stand when we are acting, then you got it wrong. You are hiding behind this pose. You don't want to deliver your audition adopting a false or silly stance that will distract the panel.

Get your head straight Literally. Tilting your head unnaturally is another 'stance' that might feel like a good thing to do but is a meaningless crutch – one that will not, finally, support quality, truthful work. Chuck it. It's a 'shield' that you get behind, an affectation, and not part of the character that you are trying to create – unless they have a neck injury. This is a dead giveaway. The panel will be wondering about that unnatural head-tilt and not focusing on you.

Chin acting Chin acting weakens your posture and strains your voice quality, neither of which is seemly or desirable. Chin-people lean forward and, bizarrely, as the chin juts forward they start to follow it. This results in a surreal forward-lean and, in extreme cases, a bending at the waist. In common with standing weirdly and head-tilting, this is clutter. You don't need it and the panel won't want it.

Chin acting is the mark of someone who doesn't trust himself and so anxiety forces him to compensate by working too hard on the wrong things. Use all this energy internally. Take a look around. When do you see people bending towards each other and jousting with their chins in conversation?

Contra-chinning exercises Use 'The Mirror' exercise and 'The Wall' to identify and eliminate this dependency. Gently place the back of your head and shoulders against the wall, and you will have no need to do anything in terms of posture and movement, so that you can just 'be' with words and meaning, with your head straight and your chin at its natural resting place. If your chin starts to jut, level it!

Burn it off! For this exercise, go through the entire speech exaggerating your chinning, or whichever tics, as wildly as you can. Get rid of them in one huge orgy of excess. But do it big, from the start to the end of the whole speech.

More about the other person Many schools are really into you 'seeing the other person'. Really get to know these other people. Know what they look like, so that visualising them is second nature by the time you get into the audition room.

Know, too, where they are in the room. Really make sure you 'set' or 'place' them very specifically. Remember to see a face not space when you do your speeches. Above all, know what your character wants of the other(s). What is that urge to communicate with someone else, and why does the urge arise?

Exercise to materialise the other people Once again, use a friend, preferably one that you have not worn out and who still likes you, to work against/with. This should help you to get a better sense of including another person.

Firstly, just do the speech to them as if they were the actual character. Later, ask your friend to try to ignore you and then to move away from you, so that you really have to work hard to maintain their attention and make them listen to you. Your character's will to speak must be greater than your mate's will to escape.

Huffing Huffing is a small, breathy escape of sound that occurs just before the 'huffer' starts to speak. It can often be witnessed in TV soaps. Huffing emanates from the desperation to prove to the audience that your character is feeling something by demonstrating this mood in a pre-emptive 'huff' of breath. This isn't good, and it also slows things down. Actors also huff to buy time enough to gather what they think the feeling/emotion is. In truth, we rarely huff in everyday life.

As I have previously proposed, moods, emotions or feelings are generated instantaneously. Your connection, therefore, needs to be instant and never demonstrated, only felt or lived-in: never huffed out. Ask a couple of people the name of their boyfriend, girlfriend or pet. As they say the name, they will experience, and you will see on their faces, an instant flood of feelings, images, memories – all very micro, very subtle, but really 'seeable'. And these will form *as* they speak. The feelings and images will also be intense and could take several minutes to describe, if you were to ask them to do so. Yet the reactions were instantaneous, free to come and go, not demonstrated and certainly not huffed.

We think at the speed of electricity. Thoughts, visions and feelings come *that* fast. When we turn a light on, it comes on as we click the switch... unless it is a neon bulb... or one of those green, low-wattage ones. Don't be low-wattage and green in your audition.

Wobbling and drifting Really work on keeping still. If you are prone to shifting and shuffling, kill the habit now. It makes the people watching feel seasick.

There is no better way to distract a panelist than by needlessly drifting around or wobbling in the space. It irritates people and also indicates that your concentration is not complete and that this disconnection is manifesting itself in random body movements. Be still, but not locked.

Even the tiniest *unintentional* movement, and I mean tiny, will tell the panel that you are fidgeting and unfocused. Any movements should be part of what's happening in your piece and not in your subconscious. I'm not saying you should deliver your offering rigor mortis-style: clearly, considered and fitting movement is entirely welcome.

Earth Exercise 'Ground' or earth yourself by simply bouncing your heels up and down a few times, making sure you feel the contact with the ground through your whole foot. If you haven't got your wobbling and drifting taped down by the time of your audition, do the bounce in the room as you are fixing your focus.

Invite someone to watch and count your wobbles. Observe someone else who is similarly afflicted in their acting and see how it detracts from what they are doing.

Leaking If you have absent-minded shuffles or wobbles, flicks, tics, eyebrows, or small or even big hand movements as you are speaking – or anything at all that happens unconsciously – then your anxieties are getting the better of you and leaking out in the form of semi-conscious movement. This also indicates that there's a part of you that is not paying total attention. Some people refer to this as 'non-verbal leakage'. If others can see your anxiety, they will feel anxious with you. If you don't show it, they won't know it!

Exercise to make you leak-proof – Burn it off Should you feel the urge for an absent-minded leak, then go for it big-time. You must *consciously* do these semi-conscious moves to the utmost and for the entirety of the speech. Exhaust them and yourself while you are at it. Purge them once and for all. Release yourself from their telltale presence. You may also get to see how daft and unconnected they are.

Exploit 'The Wall' to steady and still your mind and body. Do 'The Mirror' to spot the smaller facial leaks such as eyebrow-jerks or face-pulling. As you concentrate on just a really hot, precise vocal utterance, you might start to feel a slight impetus to t¡c. If you do, SQUASH IT! Better still, recycle the energy of ticcing into internal focus and connection.

Eye lines If the character you are speaking to is sitting or lying down, ensure that your eye line is not tilted down too much. Otherwise the panel won't have contact with you. I have seen many people talking to the seat of a chair instead of (above the backrest) where the other person's head would be, thereby rendering the other person only a few inches high. Worse, they are emoting into someone's groin. More importantly, they are alienating the panel, due to the fact that there will only be partial facial contact with the actor.

The side-on profile prolonged is not so good either. So don't put your 'other person' too side-on. If you are having a bit of a kneel in your piece, I would say it's a good plan to try and stand again as-soon-as.

End well Please don't break away as soon as the speech is done. Absolutely don't cut off and then look to the panel for approval. (Yes, really, it happens a lot.) Stay in the moment for a couple of seconds at the end of your efforts. Staying 'in it' at the end also proves and reinforces that you were connected and focused in da fursht place.

- Stop 'acting'.
- Start well – fix your focus.
- Speak, don't sing.
- Keep the flow.
- Stand well.
- Get your head straight.
- Eradicate 'chin acting' and don't huff, wobble or leak movement.
- It's all about the other person.
- Get a good eyeline.
- End well.

Performance and delivery no-nos

Coming up are some things to avoid.

Don't do spin-starts There is a notion that starting with your back to the audience, pumping up huge amounts of energy and then suddenly spinning round to start, will make things more dramatic. This only has the effect of making people jump. All of which bumps them out of the deal. As a result, they spend maybe a second and a half recovering, as opposed to being drawn into your show. Begin with your back to the panel if you wish, but bring the panel with you into your character's world. Invite, entice. That way, everyone is ready for your best work.

But... don't start by facing full-on-front, either. Be physically slightly away from, or to the side of, where you actually want to begin. Gather your focus there.

So do your prep (what you want, what the character wants, etc.) slightly side-on. Have a thought or reaction to something then maybe look up; take a pace back, forward or to the side, then start talking. If there is another character who has just been speaking, 'hear' the last words. Let these words entice or provoke your character into speaking. Maybe have a couple of thoughts or a change of mind, before speaking. We usually speak because we are compelled to. We feel the need to say what we are thinking.

Don't 'conduct' yourself Self-conducting is a habit or shield related to bobbling, shifting, chinning, etc. Conductors like to augment their speech by adding extraneous business. The hope is that doing this will further convince us of what the character is doing, saying or feeling. Conducting can also be an unconscious leakage of movement.

Some conducting can be just little, weeny hand or finger movements. But we, the audience, will still see and experience them. Particularly enthusiastic conductors can be semaphore-like in their spasms. I saw a lead guy do this to such an extent that his hands were bouncing up and down in front of him, and in the faces of whoever he was on stage with, for the entirety of the play! It made me anxious.

If you conduct:

- Your speaking and rhythms will follow the conducting.

- You will be unnatural, anxiety-ridden.

- You will not be connected.

- We will watch the movement, not you.

- Everything will be the same.

But… don't impede any movement that is natural and apt. Meet the conductor with stillness. Be calm with your body and, if you can, be motionless with your mind. Experience the words, the intentions and the meaning. No rush, no panic, no flailing.

Exercises to combat the conductor Sit on your hands and do the speech, or find a way of disabling the particular movement you are prone to.

Or, burn it off! Conduct like crazy, with huge movements, and augment these with **huge** acting for the entire speech, doing it as big as you can. Knock yourself out! Exhaust the conductor. You'll also get an idea of how dappy it looks to be doing small or large repetitive movements. Quite often, the excess of a burn-it-off exercise can release and free some interesting performance energies, too. Don't forget to rein it all back in, though.

Don't fade away at the end of your sentences! This will make you good to hear and that's an advantage. If you master this simple technical issue, your thoughts onstage, your words and your sentences, will all be empowered, interesting and quite close to thrilling. People will want to watch you and listen to you. Even if you think you sound alien or odd, get to the ends of your sentences without fading away.

You have read this in several guises now, but it is such an issue. Nearly everyone I work with reveals, initially, a fade in vocal energy and mental focus towards the ends of their sentences. People tend do this in everyday speech, but also on stage and at audition. It's a disaster, but tons of people do it *all* the time. Here's the thing: your sentences will lack oomph towards the end. They will become dull.

Having said all this, don't be a member of the upward-inflection crew?? The ones who sound like characters from Aussie soaps?? Who have rising inflections?? And say *everything* as if it was a question?? Doing this denudes everything of all meaning.

And makes you sound really dumb??

Here's a way of training yourself out of the 'fading' habit.

Exercise for faders Stand facing a wall or solid object that won't mind being poked. Stand arm's length away. Then begin to point your finger, slowly, so that as your finger finally touches the wall, your whole arm reaches full extension. As you initiate the arm movement, start speaking the line, so that both events are simultaneous and they travel concurrently. When you arrive vocally at the last word of the line, arrive physically at the wall with your fingertip. Press your finger slightly into the wall as you 'press' the last word from your lips.

The two things *must* happen together, in sync and in harmony. They must finish/arrive together. Do the whole speech like this and do it often if you suspect that you are a bit of a fader. It takes a measure of focus and coordination to get this right, but this is good for you.

A physical action in conjunction with your vocal delivery will train you to keep your energy and intention moving forward continuously through the line and to 'arrive' at its end, without dropping off or fading away.

If pressing the wall becomes tedious or sore, then extend your arm and simply point in front of you. Or you could aim for the palm of someone's hand. Just make sure there is some muscular pressure, along with vocal pressure, as you reach the peak of your 'point'. Maintain your force and intention so that they are always running steadily forward and never falling back.

It can be quite difficult to detect fading in ourselves and it's hard to hear in others, until you are tuned into it. Anything that physicalises the words and gets you to speak with energy and clarity is good.

Don't talk to the Demon Don't listen to it, either. Be in 'the now' while doing your speeches. If you engage with the Demon, you will be looking back at what just went wrong. You'll be a millisecond in the past and not in the moment.

So, a no-no round-up:

- **Don't do spin-starts.**

- **Don't conduct yourself.**

- **Don't fade away towards the ends of your sentences, thoughts or lines.**

- **Don't talk to the Demon.**

Later in rehearsals, and into the auditions

It's time to renew your energy. As you shift into this section of your campaign, you may be starting to feel a tad anxious, nervous and perhaps weary. All of these things are natural and common. But now is the time to renew your attitude and vigour.

It's crucial that you remind yourself that it is all good and nothing bad, and that fear is your friend. Use any worries or weariness you are experiencing to spur you on in your quest to do your best work, on the day.

If you let doubt, fear or frustration get to you now that you have come this far, it's a waste and it won't help. So calm it; take stock, realign and get on the case. Worry, panic and tiredness will not support your best work.

Stay strong, brave and diligent A serious campaign is a long road and often a hard trail. It is notoriously difficult to get into a drama school and if you flag at this juncture, your chances will seriously diminish. But if you are feeling fighting fit and up for it, good – hang on to this feeling and maintain your edge!

Keeping things fresh It will profit you to shake things up a little, to refresh your work and ideas from time to time. You'll gain new impetus from this injection. It is paramount, now, that you stay fresh, crisp and fragrant. Particularly if you are sweating it out at recalls. Speeches can silently deflate very easily once you have started your run of auditions, and the chances are you won't notice.

Some locos get the crazy idea that *not* engaging with the speech at this stage is a way of keeping it fresh and not wearing it out. This is a bad move. I have seen so many people return in April/May, having done a few auditions and after a refreshing holiday period, but their speeches are stale and fearful. If you don't keep working in ways that stir it up, you will go soft and floppy and you will be on autopilot, having forgotten all your connections, just bashing out the memory of a well-worn tune.

Many will tumble into denial at this stage, because they have worked *so* hard and come so far that it's scary now to discover that perhaps their performances are not peaking, nor are they as sharp in their delivery as they once were. Others dare not look at their work, in case their secret suspicions are confirmed and they have to strip everything back to basics. I completely understand this fear. It's normal. It's also natural that when you discover things have faded, you become fearful and feel a little low. You secretly dread that now you might not be as good at acting as you thought you were, or your speeches won't be as good as they have been.

Well, if this is the case, putting things right is only a matter of work and willpower. And you can do it, because you only get one shot. But should you find yourself in a flat, stale sort of state and you don't dig in and fight, you'll seriously shrink your chances.

So own up, face it and get cracking Now is the time to strip it all back to the words. Redo the exercises. Try it many ways. The people who do this at this stage are the smart, driven, conscientious ones. They are the ones who get in. If you suspect that you are losing detail and drive, act upon your suspicion. Often, it is *only* your fear of not being as good as you were last time that will stop you working. If you work, you will get better. It's that simple!

Tending to your speeches is like tending a garden: certain things grow wildly and beg a ruthless pruning. Others seek a nipping in the bud, some need a bit of 'fertiliser' – and we know how to make that. There are some that just have to be ripped out and composted. Don't be an 'unweeded garden… grown to seed'. Have nothing 'rank and gross in [your] nature', don't let it 'come to this'… Okay, enough of the *Hamlet* already.

One shot Whilst you now know that you don't have to be brilliant all the time, and getting it wrong is good, as you approach each audition day get back into a 'one shot' state of mind. Always keep exploring, but every time you run a speech, after experimenting and exploring (I promise you this will make a big difference), do it like it's the audition. Get used to hitting the sweet-spot first time out. You get one shot!

Late recaps:

- **Renew your energy and your will.**
- **Stay strong, brave and diligent.**
- **Keep things fresh by working them!**
- **You only get one shot.**

PART THREE
Practical Practice

Dealing With Shakespeare

Dealing with Shakespeare and his contemporaries (don't worry, you can do it!) If you haven't already discovered this, Shakespeare is fantastic. So try not to see his work as scary or a chore. It is merely a little bit of the unknown, the new, the strange, even difficult. The more you read and study his verse, the more you get it and the more you get from it. Shakespeare deals with everything you have ever seen, been through, thought about, wanted, loved or hated. It's about many of the things you are likely to encounter in the future. And then, he turns it all into fantastic poetry. Elegant collisions of words and ideas abound. He wizards-up rhythms, sounds, images, connections, doublings and ideas. He choreographs a cosmic waltz of words. And you get to try and dance it!

To some, especially at the very beginning, Shakespearean or classical verse may seem daunting and maybe even boring, because it is, at times, dense and removed (at first glance) from how we speak today – who we are and what we do.

Toolbox There are plenty of people more scholarly than I who have written at length and with some incisive distinction about speaking Shakespearean verse. I will not be taking them on. What I am going to do is simplify and condense things to give you the basics, so that you know what you are doing at this stage in the game. Let's face it, they will be teaching you all this in detail when you get to drama school.

What follows is a simplified and basic toolbox. Much of this will also be applicable to your modern texts.

Identify the thoughts In the lines are clues and indications as to the length of the character's thoughts. We can also ascertain the speed and, at times, the intensity of these from pointers that the writer has left within the lines, usually by the punctuation.

It is important to identify all the thoughts in the speech and to mark where they start and end, because then you know where and when to change your energy and attack. Each new thought demands new or different energy. This is the key. You shouldn't stop the flow until you get to the end of the thought or idea that your character is propounding. Thoughts are marked for you by major punctuation. Here it comes again: don't drop the vocal energy or intention until the end of the thought. Do not drop off, do not fade away. Do not pass go.

Check out the punctuation We have already had a look at punctuation in general: here are some more specific 'points'... (sorry). Classical texts use punctuation in the same sort of way that emoticons are employed today, in order to add extra meaning or to make the 'text' more demonstrative. In addition to delineating thoughts and changes, they show mood **:)** pace and hidden meaning to the actor **;)**

If, in classical texts, you encounter **! ? : ;** – use them. They are clues to help you along the way **;)** so that you don't end up **:'(** or even **:-$**

Major punctuation The full stop, the exclamation mark and often the question mark are the 'markers' for the end of a thought. But please could you *use* the question mark? And you must *use* the exclamation mark! Use them as questions and exclamations, because many students don't.

Other punctuation Commas, are not a stop, they are just a separation, or they alter the sentence/thought. You should still observe these but don't mess with the flow.

Semicolons; are not a stop, they are just an add-on to the thought and are often there to say 'and' or 'but'. They can be seen as extending the thought or making it more complex.

> And I, forsooth, in love! I, that have been love's whip; [and]
> A very beadle to a humorous sigh; [and]
> A critic, nay, a night-watch...

Colons: are not a stop. But they can, at times, be seen as representing 'because' or 'therefore' or 'it follows that'. They are there to assist a complex thought.

> All the world's a stage,
> And all the men and women merely players: [Because]
> They have their exits and their entrances;
> And one man in his time...

Make the Argument Getting a feel for the thoughts will help you to see how 'the Argument' is developing. That is to say, what the character wants and the tactics they employ to achieve this, by building their case and putting their points across. The Argument is way more interesting than the actor acting. The audience needs to be embraced by the Argument of your character, as it grows or unfolds. By which I mean they could be doing any or all of the following:

- Forming an idea.

- Defending a statement.

- Backing up an argument.

- Consolidating it.

- Concluding it.

- Deciding something.

- Realising what he/she is saying, as they speak.

New ideas and additions may pop into the Argument at any time, as the character's thought process brings new aspects and fresh impetus into play.

Sentences ending in the middle of a line If you get major punctuation in the middle of, or part-way through, a line, it is the end of the thought, but it is not quite a stop. There is a new thought or idea coming in – and fast. So you need a renewal of energy or attack. Therefore, propel yourself into the next thought, don't hang around. If there are many mid-line endings, then this is a hint from the writer that someone is talking and thinking fast – possibly even speaking for their life. For example, Hermione in *The Winter's Tale*, with the speech starting 'Sir, spare your threats…' Look at all the major punctuation coming in the middle of the lines. She's talking fast, with many complicated sentences, in much the same way as a lawyer or politician would, in order to maximise this opportunity to speak. She is, in effect, on trial and really has to get everything out before she can be interrupted. Here we see complex sentences and the telltale endings in the middle of the lines, signifying that thoughts are coming in rapidly. She is pushing through her Argument.

> Sir, spare your threats…
>   …lastly, hurried
> Here to this place, i' the open air, before
> I have got strength of limit. Now, my liege,
> Tell me what blessings I have here alive,
> That I should fear to die? Therefore proceed.
> But yet hear this: mistake me not; no life,
> I prize it not a straw, but for mine honour
> Which I would free…

Observing the 'O'

> O yet, for God's sake, go not to these wars!

> O time! thou must untangle this, not I;

The 'O' is **big**, emotional and cannot be ignored. It is not a tiny sound or word, in any sense.

Everyone (well, nearly) tries to get away with a minimum-risk, low-key 'oh' or they ignore it completely. Even now we still use this sound in many exclamatory ways:

O(h) for heaven's sake!

O(h) bloody hell!

O(h) noooo!

O – M – G!

See? We use them all the time. Don't back away, just cos they're in classical texts **:-O**

Alliteration – Assonance – Consonance Alliteration is the repetition of initial consonants for sonic effect.

...*m*uddy *m*ettl'd...

Consonance is the repetition of final consonant sounds.

...A dull an*d* mu*dd*y mettl'*d*...

Assonance is the repetition of vowel sounds in groups of words.

... wh*i*lst *I* a wh*i*le obsequiously lament...

When there are little runs of the same vowel sounds or consonant sounds, this is not a coincidence. It's a direct signal from the writer, and you should do something about them. They serve to evoke mood and atmosphere in poetry. They can sometimes be clues as to the character's state of mind. They also tell you how they are speaking. Attack them! (The sounds that is, not the characters...)

*W*as ever *w*oma*n* i*n* this humour *w*oo'd?
*W*as ever *w*oma*n* i*n* this humour *w*on?

Always / separate! If there's a word in the sentence that starts with the same letter that the previous word ended with –

...of this / straw

...all proofs / sleeping else...

...not / to these wars!

...a humorous / sigh...

– then you must **take care** to pronounce the**m m**arvelously and separate them. Note how doing this alters the attack on the words, the tone, the feeling. Also, the use of proper diction aids clarity and sense. If you run on anddon't separate, the words sounddrab and confusing, as in:

...of this traw...

– what's a 'traw'? Or:

...all proofs leaping else...

Verbs – Nouns Don't get all sexed-up about adverbs and adjectives. It's the verbs. It's the nouns. They are the ones you really want, but don't drop anything else on the way. Verbs energise. Nouns make things concrete.

Be normal – be believable Don't do a 'classical' voice. Treat things as normally as you can. Don't go into overdrive or hyper-voiced falseness. Keep it real. Keep it true.

Be believable in the way that you are speaking. Speak well, and in your own voice. Take advantage of kindly mates or do 'The Wall' and 'The Mirror' exercises to make sure you are believable and not being a bit 'Shakespeare-odd' in your delivery. Though it's also fun to have sessions when you deliberately go over the top, in order to really get hold of the words. (There's more in 'Exercises Explained'.)

Push through

(*Line of energy and intention.*)

Get to the end of the sentence.

Get to the end of the line.

Get to the end of the thought.

And again: get to the end of the line and embrace the last word. Even if you have hit the word before it, you must attack the last with the same or more energy than the one before. Don't rush the words though. I'm really simplifying all this, but at this stage you don't need to worry yourself too much with the *intricate* details of speaking verse.

The snippet below is repeated lots in this book. But I don't care.

Speak the words! Say the words clearly with great diction, with care and loving attention to every crevice of each and every word. Don't chant them. Carry them; don't drop them – any of them.

Stay strong in energy **and** intention within the words **and** pursue

this through to the last word of the **sentence and** then on to the last

word of the **line and** then on to the very last word of the **thought**.

And this is another reason why you need to identify the thoughts.

…and get on with it In general, get on with it. Don't rush things, but don't hang around. Keep the ball in the air. Keep that thought going. Don't be 'stoppy' at the end of every line. This is a common problem, sometimes for people who should know better.

Understand all the words – Part 2 Never utter words that you don't know. You really cannot blag it with Shakespeare. You have to mean something with every word and you must be coming from somewhere. In other 'words', have an idea as to what you are trying to do or convey, and why. Connect to everything you say. Make every thing and every word important. Precision. Detail. Attendance. To help you here, there are numerous glossaries and text commentaries available in hard copy or ebook and, increasingly, there are some very handy and comprehensive smartphone apps out there. You can also get books that translate or paraphrase the text into modern-speak opposite the classical text.

Shakespeare has some fantastic words or phrases. Like 'deboshed' – debauched or drunken – or 'ch'ill' – which is a vulgarism for 'I will'. Just type 'Shakespearean glossary' into your search engine and plenty of sites will pop up. While we are at it – anybody know what a 'vantbrace' is? Or what it's like to be 'mobled'? I must 'sneck up' now.

Paraphrase for clarity and greater connection Paraphrase the text into everyday speech and language use. This is a tremendously useful tool with which to dig your way into the text. Speaking the lines casually translated into modern-speak will bring home content and meaning too, by separating it from the power of the poetry. Paraphrasing takes a bit of effort, but it's worth it.

Be clear Be clear about what you are saying and about the intentions of your character. What they want. Why they speak.

Make images Have them for every word. In fact, make images and associations for all the people, places and objects you talk about. You can't really avoid this, as the writer has loaded every word with poetic image and meaning anyway.

Rhyme the rhyme If there are rhyming couplets, they cannot be ignored. They are there to hammer home what you have been talking about, in such a way as to stand out from the rest of the speech. They are there to tweak the ear of the audience, to jog them slightly.

> O time! thou must untangle this, **not I**;
> It is too hard a knot for me t'**untie**!

How big are the words? By which I mean: is the character talking about big things like suns, stars, heavens, globes, clouds, sky? Go with it. Go for it – especially when you are practising.

Other clues and hints Look for repeated words, themes and imagery. These are no accident:

> To whom should I complain? Did I *tell* this,
> Who would believe me? O perilous *mouths*,
> That bear in them one and the self-same *tongue*,

Also, look for opposites – antithesis:

> That, he had twenty heads to *tender down*
> On twenty blocks, he'll *yield* them *up*,

> Hooking both *right* and *wrong* to the appetite,

> Then, *Isabel*, *live* chaste, and, *brother*, *die*:

Are there comparisons at play?

> *He* was the mark and glass, copy and book,
> That fashion'd others. And *him*, O wondrous *him*!
> O miracle of men! *him* did *you* leave,
> Second to none, unseconded by *you*,

The same applies to smut and innuendo; it really is there on purpose. You are not imagining it. Make the connections:

> My cherry lips have often kissed thy stones...

Or:

> MARIA. A mark marvellous well shot; for they both did
> hit it.

> BOYET....Let the mark have a prick in't, to mete at, if it
> may be.

Oooooh – some assonance in there too :)

- Identify the thoughts by reading the punctuation.
- Make the argument.
- Kick on when you get to a mid-line ending.
- AlwayS / Separate.
- Speak normally – don't 'sing' the words.
- Get to the end of the line, don't fade in energy or attention.
- Get on with it – but don't rush. Stay in each word.
- Understand what you are saying. Look it up. Find out.
- Paraphrase for clarity and connections.
- Be clear.
- Make images for the words.

Your Song

If you enjoy a good sing-song and you are a decent singer, fantastic. But many candidates who feel that they are not strong singers tend to whip themselves into a bit of a fear-frenzy over the fact that they are required to choose and tunefully convey a song. Drama schools want to hear your singing voice at an acting audition for several reasons. Your singing voice will give them a better idea of your vocal strength, range and general skills. The song is also a way of giving you an opportunity to show yet another side to what you can do in another format.

Most people are vocally trainable and that, after all, is what you are seeking at drama school – more training. So here's the good news:

don't fret too hard about your singing but, if you are concerned, you can do something about it.

The main thing is that the panel will just want to hear that your voice is okay and that you can hold a tune. So don't get into a tizz if you're not a top-notch tenor or you don't have a repertoire of songs to draw on.

There are numerous stories of people having been successful just by singing 'Happy Birthday', and they may be true. But I wouldn't ever recommend that you do this, because it will show a lack of thought and preparation. Anyway, these paragraphs will give you a positive and confident plan of action.

Choosing it When selecting your song, apply the same criteria that you did when selecting texts for acting:

- Does it suit your age, playing and singing range?

- Does it 'speak' to you? Is there room for change and is there a journey for the character?

Pick lyrics and tunes that will be fun or interesting to hear and that carry a good story or journey for the character. Don't get seduced by tragic or overly emotive tunes.

Pop songs don't really give you the opportunity to connect and journey. Soul songs and blues numbers are good, but often quite tricky to sing. Watch out for overly repeated lines – they can be hard to keep fresh and, without a backing band, you may get boring.

Contrast it Don't forget about contrast. If you can, choose a song to contrast with your speeches in terms of mood, tone and character, then you are already providing them with more and fresh evidence of your range and abilities. You are also proving that you have done the work and thought about things.

Working with the text Work on the text of the song in the ways I have already suggested with regard to your monologues. Get your head around the fact that, just because this is a song, it doesn't mean you can skip the study. You should know where it is from, who wrote it and the background to the words, their meaning and why it may have been written. Approach all this in exactly the same way as I have set down for acting work.

Giving your delivery an edge So, bearing in mind that you don't necessarily need to be a brilliant singer, here are some things for you to do, so that you maximise your effectiveness and mollify any trepidation about this part of your audition or recall.

- Select a number that you like and that suits you.

- Who is the person singing?

- Why they have opened their mouth in the first place?

- Where are they? A sense of place really helps vision and delivery.

- Start well: don't just leap into the words, the sounds and the rhythms without true understanding and connection. Create the world.

- If you are singing unaccompanied (most drama-school acting courses are unaccompanied), find the note in your head first. Doing this will diminish the risk of starting too high or too low. Don't just begin without thinking about that first note.

- In contrast to the way you deliver your speeches, you should perform the song in its original accent or dialect. If you can uncover one written in your own accent, fine. But it is important to sing in the written accent of the song. Again, work with your background and ethnicity, not against it.

- Don't assume the start of the song is the best place for you to begin. The panel may only want to hear a few bars, so make sure you pick the section that sells your voice the best! If they do only listen to a few bars and stop you, don't judge or wonder why. Onwards! It's all good and nothing bad. Don't let this interfere with whatever they require you to do next.

• Choose something that you can connect to in performance. It is so much more effective to be reflective and internal than to treat the panel as a cabaret audience.

But:

If you really, truly are a singing disaster zone Go for something big and brash like 'Big Spender', 'New York, New York' or 'Consider Yourself'. In this instance, selecting loud and proud options will show that you have courage and are not afraid of showing off what might be perceived as being your weaker area.

The panel will be interested to see if you can sell any piece of text, so: *if to sing is not your thing – pick loud and proud.*

One student (who was not the most gifted of singers) chose a comedy number by the actor and comedian Bernard Cribbins. He just went for it in terms of delivery and attitude. The panel loved it. This courageous and different line of thought really served him well. He stood out for the right reasons.

If you really can't sing, or at least have convinced yourself that you can't, then you have to address this by singing more! They will be working on your voice extensively if you get into drama school. So get ahead, start now. Join a choir! Go to church, even. Have some singing lessons?

If you deal with it, the spectre of having to sing will not be hanging over you and interfering with your acting work. The best way to diminish worry is to deal with the cause of it.

I have included a song list in the Appendix.

Exercises Explained

Here are some more detailed descriptions of the exercises I have been mentioning, plus extra ones. At any point in your journey, using exercises will help you to:

- Mine the text.

- Experiment with possibilities.

- Get physical.

- Explore the words.

- Check for and crush tics and technical bad habits.

Exercises will set you free to run the speeches, shielded from the **stress** of having to be *good*, without the pressure of having to remember everything. Using exercises takes you out of the 'rush' of performing the speech and creates a rest area, away from the hurly-burly of trying to perfect a full-on performance. In rehearsal it's so easy to cook up a storm of stress by having to cope with:

- Trying to remember this.

- Not forgetting that.

- Getting through the line.

- Slowing down, speeding up.

- Speaking well.

- Not dropping lines or words.

- Remembering to stand well.

- Having images for the words

...and all the million other things that you have to ingrain on your psyche. This can feel like way too much pressure. So exploit the liberating qualities of exercises, manoeuvres and distractions to chill sometimes. Maybe tackle one thing at a time, without the onrushing train that your audition piece can become. Do your thing from time to time in the calm of the waiting room, before getting back on the train.

The Wall

This is a more detailed explanation of 'The Wall' exercise. Using 'The Wall' will get you to centre on the words and meaning by stopping you from thinking about your body, as opposed to many of the exercises so far, which have been all about experiencing text via the body. 'The Wall' can diagnose and treat many ailments.

- Stand, relaxed, with your shoulders and the back of your head resting on a flat, vertical surface. Make sure that your shoulders are at rest there too. Keep them there throughout, but make sure that you are not uncomfortable. Keep that chin down.

- Your heels ought to be about four or five inches out from the wall. Now when you run your speech, there is nothing else to worry about. It's just you and the words and your voice. The rest of *you* is rendered physically and mentally still, by the wall.

- Now you can turn your attention to identifying and mending the vocal and delivery issues that I have been talking about so far.

- You are also able to focus on your body to calm twitches, face-pulling and other unnecessary 'leaks' and movement. You'll soon pick up how great the tendency is to move or fidget while you are speaking.

- On the wall, it is possible to detect the urge to tic at the very emergence point of these tics even if they are tiny. Chop them all out while at the wall. You don't have to worry about anything else. That's the simple beauty of it. Do it often and decide what you need to look for each time. 'The Wall' gives you *time* and *space* away from the hurly-burly of performing, to evaluate and connect.

The Mirror

This is not for everyone and you must take care to use it prudently. Delivering the speech to yourself in the mirror is an old one. However, if you use this judiciously it can pay off, as long as you don't start to hate yourself or disappear in a fruitless, narcissistic, or paranoid puff.

Combined with 'The Wall', 'The Mirror' should reveal all the bad habits and delivery faults that I have set down so far. You have to scale down the size of the performance, but keep the intention and the intensity.

Use your reflection as a vigilant but friendly monitor, not a harsh critic. Have your monitor make you go back and address the things that are fake.

This should be a calm time, with just you and the spirit of your work. Banish anxiety. Eject the Judge. Kill the Demon.

Other things to fix using 'The Wall' or 'The Mirror'

- **Stand and deliver... the truth** Stand close and deliver the words as truthfully and clearly as you are able.

- **Stop and fix – be nice** Stop and start again if you detect falsehoods or a lack of precision or connection. Concentrate on fixing, not berating, yourself. Be nice, don't demonise or get frustrated. But be meticulous, let nothing slip by you.

- **Face-pulling** Use these exercises to detect and eliminate face-pulling, eyebrow-raising and chin acting. Keep your face motionless at the mirror or the wall. Things get real then. Don't 'make emotion' on/in your face – if it is there feel it in your soul, but don't show it to us! Internalise and *reuse* face-pulling energy and urges.

- **Talk, don't sing** You know this by now, *talk* the lines, *say* the words – don't sing, chant or intone. Make sure you are 'on voice' and using performance power. Do you hear the truth?

- **Truth** Ask yourself if you believe you. Is there truth in your connections? Are you 'vocalising emotion'? Trying to simulate or even generate emotion (fear, sadness, grief, tears), simply by making those noises and sounds *in* your voice? This is not the truth. These things need to come from somewhere deeper. They cannot be manufactured in your vocal sounds. Is your face true?

- **Skipping on** Don't reach for the next thought or words until you have finished those that you are on. This is another common fault and it signifies that the actor is rushing, not giving each and every word its weight. If you rush, you 'skim' off the surface of things.

NB. Your face is perfect for the job. *Your* voice is perfect, so don't screw them!

Use another body

Engage the services of relative, friend or fellow performer to help you find-and-fix the issues mentioned above, and explore these points below:

- **Scale and distance** Communicate the text to them at various distances, incrementally adjusted. Start in someone's ear, then increase the gap. Go to one or two metres, then ten, then maybe thirty.

If you are prone to under-doing things, have them stand further away. This will help you to project your voice and intentions. If you tend to overdo things, invite them up close. Always ask if they believed you. Just mix it up and experiment with what different distances can do. Explore intimacy vs. remoteness, small performance vs. big.

- **Attention** Ask your helper to move around the space while avoiding you. Meanwhile, you attempt to get up in their face, to really *tell* them what you have to say.

- **Obstruction** Fix a point to move towards in the space, then have them hold you back bodily or somehow deflect you from your destination. Don't be diverted from the speech or the character's wants and intentions.

- **Propulsion** This can be physical propulsion, or you can do it by gestures and signals. Or your helper might use vocal encouragement: 'Come on, come on! Faster, slow down, what? What? Get on!' And other such *helpful* comments…

Your job is to respond to their suggestions, while maintaining all the connections. Your partner can gently shove you around in the space while you resist or allow the shove. How do you feel? They don't have to just shove; they can lead or guide you.

How does this affect the words?

- **Blindfold guide** Wear a blindfold while they lead you through the space. This aspect can seriously change or affect both mood and reactions to words and ideas. It can be extremely liberating. You have no other responsibility. There's just you, the dark, the words and the travelling.

Get physical

Getting physical just before or during a speech can really make a significant impact on the outcome. Try:

* A few press-ups.

* A short run, if only up and down the stairs.

Or:

* Do couple of star-jumps.

* Push against someone or something.

All of these will have an effect on the energy and rhythm of what you are doing.

Give yourself another focus

Often, diversionary tasks will take you to places that your ego, or the Demon, may have prevented you from visiting. Try your stuff while doing other things like:

* Washing up.

* Pumping up, in the gym.

* Riding on the bus (dare you!?).

* Brushing your teeth.

* Bouncing a ball.

* Walking fast, or walking backwards or sideways.

'Dances'

I have used 'dancing' many times in workshops to help students relate to the words and content of text in an abstract way, so that they can then express moods, rhythms and emotional reactions in a heightened, physical context. (Don't worry, you don't need to be any good at it.) The idea here is to find the punctuation and rhythms written into the text and then to experiment with them.

At first, you should stick to what appears to be the writer's rhythm. As the exercise develops, expand and free up your movement while discovering what feelings and emotions come to you from the words. Eventually, and ideally, a wild, interpretative dance should emerge – a fun dance that liberates the words and feelings for you. Just try the next 'step' and see how it goes.

a. Start with a step, slide, shuffle

So: commence gently and simply. An interesting way to probe the punctuation further and physicalise the text is to 'shuffle' the rhythm of modern pieces, or the meter/iambics of classical pieces, with a little foot shuffle for each syllable or beat:

So / youwould, / ifyouwished, / needtotakeafootshuffle / .

Step / stepstep, / stepstepstep, / stepstepstepstepstepstep / .

Or by sliding the soles of your feet, so that each move is a slide or shuffle:

foreverysyllable, / andeveryburstofactivity / . Okay?

slideslideslideslideslideslide, /
slideslideslideslideslideslideslideslide / . Slideslide?

- **Be accurate** The footwork *must* drive the words from your mouth. You cannot step then speak. The sounds have to come up from the floor, via the feet, through the body. The two actions are simultaneous, but the tendency is to allow the mouth to drive the words, so attend!

This is tricky and quite tiring, but great for letting the words into the body. It's also good for learning them neutrally, as opposed to following a pattern that you set in your head. You can then get closer to the writer's rhythms, and thus to those of the character.

- **Explore the staccato – then loosen it!** The words and moves will, of necessity, start out very staccato and false as you shuffle them out. This is good. Do it a few times more like this, then get to work on loosening the staccato so that things get more natural and real-sounding, but still driven by the feet. Listen out for the sounds played on the floor.

- **In silence – bury the words** To truly experience the rhythms and sounds made by your feet, don't say the words aloud now. Just keep them going in your head while you shuffle out the footwork.

b. Salsa

- **Bigger moves** As you get looser and more natural, you can ease your foot movements and begin to translate these up through your legs and body.

- **Experiment** Slowly experiment with the rhythms you find. Your slides now become bigger moves, as you develop a whole-body dance in a salsa or rumba stylee, or whatever works for you!

- **Grow it** The rhythms and the way you deal with the words should grow accordingly. You should not seek to impose *your* rhythms; let them grow organically from those that you originally discovered.

- **Feel it** Begin now to feel reactions to and within what you are doing. Expand and explore moves and feelings.

- **Lose the words** 'Dance' the speech out, but speak the words only in your head. Listen to the sounds and rhythms of your feet on the floor.

- **Let rip** Let rip!

c. Contemporary

Now that you have a funky thing happening with your body, words and movement, you can go for the contemporary dance of your speech.

- **Imagine** Express and exploit all the gestures, postures, jumps, rolls, twists and turns that come to you. Unlock the whole thing in wild, physical expression of the text. The music for your dance, and the tempos, are now all in the words and in your imagination. Let these things work on you. Really melt bodily into the highs and lows, the ebbs the flows of feelings, energies, sounds and rhythms. Push them. Extrapolate.

- **Audibly lose the words** Do *your* dance speaking the words in your head or maybe while just muttering the words. But be sure to let the words affect you.

This may all sound a bit arty and nuts. That's cos it is. But it really works for lots of people.

Some find it easier to fire up this stage if they start lying down, then build in bodily reactions until they are on their feet. Whatever. It doesn't matter. Just don't be scared: this is one thing you really can be absolutely terrible at, you can just do it for the hell of it, without having to come up with the perfect goods or a decent dance.

One-word build-up

This offers you the luxury of time to encounter each phrase one word at a time and get to know the feel of the words in your mouth while you forge a mental image to accompany each one. It will also train you to maintain the ongoing flow of each line. Build the whole line, one word at a time. Then go on to the next line, then the next and so on. This could take a while to get through.

To

To be,

To be, or

To be, or not

To be, or not to

To be, or not to be

To be, or not to be: that

To be, or not to be: that is

To be, or not to be: that is the

To be, or not to be: that is the question

Then say the whole line:

To be, or not to be: that is the question:

Don't be choppy or staccato when you say each completed line. Be natural.

Keep an equal or increasing momentum and weight, always heading for that last word while never letting the momentum and energy fall. Come back to this regime if and when you sense that you are losing the flow, momentum or feel of the words in the lines.

This exercise should then extend to cover the length of entire thoughts. Some people use an arm movement to describe the 'arc' of a thought.

While you are at it Look at and say all the last words of the lines, in this case:

Question
Suffer
Fortune
Troubles
Sleep
End
Shocks
Consummation
Sleep

And so on…

Get hold of them. Chew them. Mull them. Know them. These are where the line is headed, and where you and the line will arrive. They will also unlock the speech for you, unfolding the mood, content and even the intention of the speech and the character. These words are where, vocally, you need to head for.

PART FOUR
The Auditions: Winning Ways – and Knowledge

All in the mind

In these next sections, there will be recurrent reminders of stuff that has been covered, but they are pertinent to each specific stage of the game in your campaign and they are there in case you are visiting these pages in isolation. There's also new information.

Okay, if you are a week or so away from your first audition, then it's time to get mentally strong for the event. Remember, nerves are good, excitement is good; action over inaction is really good.

Besides anticipating the fruition of all your efforts and exercises so far, you should remind yourself of a number of the things that have rippled through these pages. So let's revisit:

Mantras Revisited

I have added a couple which might be of use to you at this stage of the game.

1. Mantras for the head

It's all good and nothing bad Whatever happens in the run-up to the audition, and indeed during it, keep hanging on to 'It's all good and nothing bad.' Positive vibe. Always.

Be a Warrior, not a Worrier If you only worry, or if you just dither and panic, you get nowhere and nothing can be done.

Make fear your friend You are, inevitably, going to be nervous. But harness this force and turn it into something positive and galvanising. Make it work for you, not against you. Maintain a gentle focus on what you want to achieve, which is...

It's not about drama school – I am just here to do my best work Don't ever think about the audition as 'I *have* to get into drama school.' Just look forward to the opportunity to do your best work and possibly even enjoy a moment of release for all the hard effort and thought you have been putting in. Having said this, it is also true that...

You only get one shot So you don't want to blow it. You need to be mentally strong and cool-headed enough to step up to the plate, take a second or so to remind yourself of what is required for you to do your best work, create the world, then go! But make sure you can accomplish everything you want to, first time round. Now is the time get cracking again on hitting the bullseye in one shot. So start well!

Be you, be true – again, yes I know, but... You have to be who you are, not dwindled and small because the auditioners are **big** and they have what you are after. No, no. They want to meet the real you, maybe the slightly nervous you, but 'you' nonetheless.

2. Mantras for the work

Start well, end well It is absolutely fundamental that you make certain you are getting your focal points right before you start your speeches. Are you setting your focus? Are you connecting to the world of the character?

Get used to going from one speech to the other whilst staying centered. No matter how well or badly you think it went, it is always 'all good and nothing bad'. You have no idea what the panel thought, so don't think or judge for the panel – it's a waste.

Change is good! You've read it often, but it is crucial. Keep the panel engrossed and interested. Use change and use it frequently. Don't stay locked on to one thing, or on one level. Change brings life and colour, excitement and interest.

Be specific with words and intentions Never be general with what you are doing. Take care of the detail of what the character means. To be specific, you always have to be on duty while you rehearse and always when auditioning. Staying on duty takes diligence.

Go anywhere, but come from somewhere Be free and open enough to go where the moment takes you, but make sure what you are doing and saying is rooted in truth and depth.

It's all about the words The words are all you have. Your job is to deliver them with credibility and clarity. Explore them. Respect them. Let them affect you. You should not try to affect them. They are not yours to do that with.

Make the speech about the other character And about what yours wants from them. 'Place' the other character in the space; see them, hear them, address them. **See a face, don't just see space** when addressing another character.

Lighten up, have fun Don't be so scared, defensive, hyped or serious that the panel never sees who you are. They need to have a good time too.

What Happens at an Audition?

Well, all auditions vary slightly in their content and nature, but one thing is for certain: your auditioners are not there to persecute you or drag you through any kind of horrid ordeal. Most candidates report having had a warm, fun encounter. They met staff and students who were genuinely interested in them as people. Some first auditions are group events, others will be just you and the panel. If it's a group session, there could well be a group warm-up. Do a conscientious warm-up to help you loosen up. The school is already looking at you. But relax, too. (See 'Group Auditions'.)

For detailed information about what will happen at each school and first-hand feedback from candidates' personal experiences over the years plus loads of other stuff, click onto this book's website: www.excellentauditions.co.uk

Introductory talk Sometimes an introductory talk is given about acting, the profession and the particular school you are at. They may ask if you have any questions. Do you? Is it a real one?

Waiting around There will often be some waiting to do. Current students might be on hand to look after you and show you around. Some are chattier than others. This is a good opportunity to ask questions. But don't blow all your concentration completely on chatting. There could be a waiting area. Chill, but 'maintain' in this space, whilst steering round distractions. Some auditions can be a bit in-and-out and it's all over before you know it. So tune in to what you want to achieve. One shot!

The panel and the room The panel typically consists of between two and four people, sometimes with an ex- or current student there, too. The rooms can vary in size, shape and ability to intimidate. Therefore, feel the space as you go in. Adapt to it. Tame it. Own it. Feel good.

Interview It's possible that they will want to talk to you before the speeches, or after – or both. If they want to have a chat beforehand, see that you don't get too cosy. Give yourself time to get back into gear before you start your monologues (see 'The Interview').

Song Some might want you to do your song; others will wait until you are recalled.

Recordings It's becoming common for schools to record auditions. Ignore the camera, unless you get instructions to the contrary. Don't be fazed – it's just machinery.

Re-direction The staff might (or might not) rework your pieces. Be ready, but don't expect it or worry about either outcome. Re-direction could be down to several reasons:

- To verify that you have other gears.

- To see if you are wedged into one well-practised mode and incapable of change or plasticity.

- To experience collaboration with you.

- To find out if you are a listener.

- They just want to see more of what you can do.

Typically, the panel could request you to sit down, tone it down and redo the monologue directly to them. Here, they will be monitoring your ability to connect with the passage, rather than to act it out. Other auditioners could ask you to do the opposite of what you just gave them, or they might set a scene for you. For example:

> Imagine you are lying to someone who you really like because you don't want to give them bad news.

If you have had an experimental journey with your pieces, re-direction will not present a problem for you.

'I have found over the last few days that it is not the actual audition that has been on my mind but small, trivial things, such as what I should wear and how to greet the panel at the beginning of the audition.' Alice

Group auditions

A group audition is very much about how you interact with the other candidates.

You will probably do your pieces in front of everyone else as well. If you are asked to go first or last – it's all good…

'Basically, relax and don't try to be someone you are not, but be willing to try whatever they may throw at you. For example, during one audition I was asked to be a sparkler! In this situation, don't act like you think this is stupid (even though it is, really), but just embrace it, have fun and don't take yourself too seriously. And stay focused at all times, as the panel may call you in suddenly because someone may not have turned up or something. Do not waste time scaring yourself or letting others scare you.' Dani

OMG, they are all better than me! Don't compare other people's work to your own. Just go with the experience. When you see someone else respond to an idea or create a moment, you might well be staggered by their inventiveness and blown away by their skill. This is when you start to judge your own efforts against theirs and begin to think that you are rubbish.

You can bet your bottom dollar that the person who has just staggered you will be thinking exactly the same thing about you. We all do this. It's human nature. So don't worry. Stay positive. Everyone around you may look fab; they could be doing rave speeches and being really creative and witty in the impro stuff. Worse still, they might be getting all the exercises right, seemingly with no effort at all. Don't worry, because they are not you and they cannot offer what you do. It's all good and nothing bad. If, perchance, a candidate is awful, don't bring negative waves into your head or the room. Be generous.

Support the work in the room! Collective effort and shared focus are the essences of how a piece of theatre is conceived and performed. Support the work in the room by being attentive to and interested in what everyone else is doing. That is what the school is looking for. If you fidget through other people's efforts and switch off when it's not your turn, it's a dead giveaway that you're not a team player. Depressingly, many participants just down tools when the attention isn't on them. Don't be one of these. Support the work!

It's all about the work Many group auditions and recalls are designed to present you with the work ethic and general ethos of the school, so workshops will echo the principles and philosophy of their training regime.

Get into what they want you to do. Make it about that. Don't worry about you or how you are doing. Have a great time interacting and learning a shed-load more than you already knew. For this day, you'll have some of the best teachers in the country, possibly the world.

> 'Group auditions are like nothing you expect. I thought everyone else auditioning would be judging the way I look, as well as the panel, but it really is silly to think like that. It's better to just focus on yourself and not wrap yourself up in everyone else's judgements. But obviously you will be working with them too. Not to enter as a nervous wreck is good too. Haha.' Steph

The Interview

Generally speaking, candidates approach the interview in one of two ways. Either they do nothing about it, because they don't see it as important. Or they get into a right old flap and become terrified, thereby making this part of the process into a massive mountain of dread and self-doubt.

If you fall into the former category, then the next paragraph should be a wake-up call. If you are in the latter – relax. The interview is just a friendly chat and the interviewers are not there to grill or fry you.

The contact you have with the panel is important; it is just as important as the audition.

This is where the panel will wish to see who you are, discover what you think and generally find out about you. Other factors might include:

- How **committed** you are to drama-school training and the ensuing career.

- They could want to test your **character** with more probing questions and comments.

- They will be interested to see if you can **speak** with authority about your choices.

- They will want to know if you can be **objective** when discussing your performance.

- They may be keen to hear if you **know** what's happening out in Theatreland.

- Do you have a finger on the pulse of the **profession** that you want to enter?

Like I said, these encounters are usually warm and amicable, sometimes funny, often interesting exchanges of ideas. But to maximise your chances, you must not underestimate the significance of this element of the audition.

What else do the interviewers want to know? Here are some of the more salient points:

- Are we going to be able to **work** with this person?

- Are they **listening**?

- Are they going to be positive and not negative? **Open** to suggestion?

- Are they going to be **fun**?

- Can they **hack it**?

- Can they **do** the hours?

- Are they **precious**?

- Are they **committed**?

- Are they personable, **affable**, sociable?

- Can they **collaborate**?

- Are they interested in the **art** and the profession?

- Or only interested in **themselves**?

It's not an exam: how to respond to a comment or question Well, it's a cinch really – Relax! By now you have read this a lot: you just need to be you – perhaps a teeny bit more energised and attentive than usual, but you. What's important is that you make real contact and communicate properly and clearly. Don't get all formal and rigid, as if the interview were some sort of exam.

Talk *with* them. Be even, but not flat. Give yourself time to think about the real answer to the question. The panel really won't mind waiting for a considered response.

Seek balance. You don't want to be so laid-back that you slouch around in the chair looking cool. Conversely, you don't want to be on-the-edge-of-your-seat hyper-keen – like a little doggie.

Mind the gap! Don't jump in – stand back. The one thing that people usually want to do in an interview, especially if they have dwindled themselves, is to leap in with 'noise' to fill that terrible gap between when the interviewer finishes talking and it becomes their turn. Don't just jump. Take time to assimilate the comment or words. This is proper, normal conversation.

Listen to them by shutting down the inner voices Kill the demons! These inner voices may be saying things like, 'Do I look like I'm really listening?' 'How can I be keener?' 'I'm nodding, but I haven't really heard much of what they said.' 'Please like me!'

If you don't understand what is being said to you, give yourself some time by repeating what was said or asked. Then you can think. You could ask them to clarify. It's much better to communicate properly. Make it a conversation with them, not with yourself.

Rubbish answers and hole-digging If you are talking nonsense, or your argument turns to gibberish halfway through, admit it and change your answer. You don't *have* to keep on with a rubbish answer just because you started out with it.

This would be as foolish as pushing on with a poor performance just because your piece started that way or slipped into it. Rescue things! Take control of your destiny! Don't dig more holes. Own up and start again. Say, 'Actually, that's rubbish and not what I wanted to say. This is what I really meant…'

Then say what you really wanted to say before panic kicked in and you started talking sh*te. The panel will admire your honesty.

If you don't know, say so There could be instances where you have never thought about what is being asked, or you genuinely don't know. The almost irresistible urge is to blag it. That is the first instinct, the panic instinct. Don't blag it! Tell them you have never actually thought about this, then offer an opinion. This is smart, because then you won't dig holes or force yourself to make a rubbish answer. Also, they won't be able to toss you digging implements to make the hole bigger – because you are not in 'the hole.'

Rambling Nerves or uncertainty may make you ramble on. Keep it tight. If you have answered the question or made your point, stop talking. That's it. Finish. Stop.

Be open, be honest, be you, be true Just try to be open and honest. The school will warm to courage, honesty and openness. They like people who are committed and focused. But they also want to work with fun, generous types who are able to communicate effectively with directors, tutors or fellow students.

What's the answer? There is not necessarily a right or wrong answer – *just your answer*. I could go on here about what the best or preferred answers might be, but this would be defeating the object, which is for you to consider what you feel about a statement or question from someone on the panel. Then, after thinking, you can make a considered, honest response.

To be *honest*, if you are truly serious about things, if you've done your research and approached your pieces with integrity, you will already know the answers to most of them. Even the nasty ones like: 'What can you offer us?' or 'What can we offer you?'

Likely questions At the back of this book, I have put together some samples of commonly asked questions, so that you can familiarise yourself. Mull them over. But don't come up with an automatic, pre-learned answer. I've also made a few notes as to what some of the questions are about and how to approach them.

> **Question marks:**
>
> * Have a proper conversation.
>
> * Don't jump in with an answer just to fill the silence.
>
> * Listen and understand.
>
> * If you don't know, say so! Then offer an opinion.
>
> * Don't dig holes.
>
> * Be as honest as you can.
>
> * Don't ramble: answer the question, then stop.
>
> * The panel will appreciate *your* answer.

Vital prep approaching the audition day

Be strong, get fit As well as being mentally strong, you should also consider your physical fitness, because many schools have all-day, physical-workshop-type auditions. If you are recalled, you will, more than likely, be involved in physical classes, some of which are very exacting.

Preview that interview Buff up on what you have been up to lately. Consider jobs, experiences, adventures, shows you've been to see. Readdress the reasons why you want to train as an actor.

Walk in well Here is a really fun, but quite scary, exercise to help you get ready to walk in and meet the panel, calmly but positively.

'Hi, I'm Jane Smith and I am talented.'

You won't really want to say *that* on the day, but this exercise is a way of revealing your shields and tics.

'I'm talented' is an uncomfortably difficult thing to say: no one wants to walk into a room and proclaim, arse-like, that they are talented. It seems boastful. And many people don't have the self-esteem even to think this thought. But when you audition or do an interview, you should at least *feel* talented, thanks to your fantastic prep. It's what you have to do with your presence and manner, while still being amenable and normal.

This (fun) exercise is great preparation for the moment when you have to walk into a room under public pressure, without trying to hide behind fidgeting or flirting or making all manner of mad moves. It also acts a micro-audition piece that you have to connect to. It is a short text that you have to deliver truthfully, and conclude well.

- Gather some auditioning friends or drama classmates.

- One by one, walk into the space, step up onto a chair or stand in front of your pals.

- Take a second to take them all in and 'be' with them all, genuinely and warmly.

- Then say, really truthfully:

  'Hello/hi, I'm Andy Johnson and I'm talented.' [Say your own name... obviously...]

- Do this calmly, and as 'you'. Without leaning, chinning, worrying, lying, fidgeting, drifting or compensating. Don't 'act' it, 'dwindle' it, or overcompensate it.

- Don't change your voice up or down. Don't fade or tail off towards the end of this very short sentence. Everyone else will be tuning in very carefully to scan for these telltale things.

- Ask the others if they believe you. By 'believe', I mean were you... just you? Were you as truthful and honest with yourself as you could be, vocally, mentally and physically?

- The feeders-back must gently (or, for more fun, un-gently) note every little untruth or fidget. They must be honest, look deep and then tell all. This can a very taxing exercise, especially if the rule is that you have to keep doing it all again if, in the opinion of your 'panel', you screwed it up. But it can be hysterically funny, if done in the right spirit, to see the idiocy and contortions we invent to try to hide ourselves or avoid being 'seen'. And this is a paradox, considering acting is fundamentally about being stared at.

Do this exercise with generosity to the people watching and to yourself. Be nice to be with. Do it well, not aggressively, not overconfidently or cockily, or shyly. Be still. Be confident within yourself.

The night before

Embrace any feelings you have and fix your mind on what you want to achieve.

Sort out the clothes that you know are right for this day. Dress properly in working gear.

All schools stipulate sensible clothing. Take out any piercings: never go with a tongue piercing in. I know! – but it happens. The secret is to get them to focus, undisturbed, on you and what you are doing so they can see how dazzling you are. You don't want them dazzled by jewellery glittering, or sidetracked by crazy designs, terribly funny T-shirts, or un-sensible shoes.

You require their undivided attention so you can do your thing. Don't have the panel wondering what statement you think you're making about yourself with the pierced eyeball, or the fedora hat. Dress neutral – but not like a mime artist.

Pack your stuff Maps, books, sheet music if required, MP3 player, phone, water, change, things to keep your hair off your face.

Include whatever you need to keep you comfortable. Find something warm to wear between classes. Just don't be hoofing around in the morning looking for things.

What have you been up to? Get thinking on how to talk about what you have been doing lately. This can be a common conversation topic. Have you read anything interesting lately? Seen any shows? Who was in them? Who directed them? What about the designer? Don't forget to include things you might have done outside acting, like your shoe-shop job, or that intensive chicken-training course.

Have a look at the list of interview questions (at the back of the book) Play some inspiring music and browse through a few questions. Shun prepped, fixed answers but know the area you could talk about without 'um'-ing and 'er'-ing.

Don't party the night before (you'd be surprised...) Instead, re-read their prospectus so that the image of the school, and what they are about, is clear in your mind, and you can answer questions such as 'Why do you want to come here?' or 'What can we offer you?'

Don't wonder and wander Try to relax. Don't fill your head with panic and conjecture. It's okay to be nervous. Accept the nerves, don't luxuriate in them. Go for a walk or a swim. Take a bath. Treat yourself somehow. Have an early night.

Run your speeches Start well, fix your needs and those of the character. Connect and do your best work.

Night-before-caps:

- Pack what you need, so that you are not rushing in the morning.

- Refresh your memory as to what you have been up to lately.

- **Check over the interview questions. Peruse your personal statement.**
- **Don't fill your head with worry.**
- **Run your speeches. Run a bath.**

'I never felt ready, but I never felt unprepared. What I think about is the interview, the body language I'm showing them and how to refine my enthusiasm so that I don't look like that naive and immature girl who has been in a couple of plays at school and thinks she can take a stab at it in the real world.' Luci

The audition day

Try to have fun. Go there with the idea of having a good time. Enjoy the opportunity to let rip with everything you have learned. Meet some interesting people on the panel.

'So yeah, the usual feelings are all there: nervous, excited, scared sh*tless, etc., but get out of your own head and you realise it isn't about worry. It's about focus and positivity. And… That's about it :D' Dani

Banish panic – make fear your friend (revisited) Right, because today is 'the day', you are going to be nervous. You are going to be afraid. There is nothing you can do about that. So embrace the nerves; make them work *for* you, not against you.

What's the point of letting these feelings ruin your fantastic-ness? What's the point of buying into other people's anxiety? I'll tell you: none – there is no point. Big tip: the panel members really do know that you're nervous and they are used to this. They make allowances.

Nerves are a large part of the performance buzz. They are natural. Professional actors get them all the time. They are part of the thrill and the adrenaline of the situation. That's why acting is attractive. The risk. The thrill. The danger. Let nothing get in your way. You've come this far, now go for it! It's all good and nothing bad.

Wake up early, but chill out Today, especially this day, don't get up and start doing 'getting in to drama school' dramas. Don't make this your goal for the day: it will render things desperate. Sure, this is your aim. But really, you want to be preparing yourself and your mind for the act of doing your best work when it counts most. If you let anything get in the way of that, after all your hard work, you are crazy. Some of the things that follow will help arm you and make you strong for the day.

Look back at the mantras Carry them with you for the day.

Eat a decent breakfast You'll need the energy, if it's a day-long audition or a recall where there are likely to be a lot of physical demands. Take carbs with you.

Do a vocal warm-up Do this either at home or on the way, but do it. Don't worry about looking stupid. This is an important element in ensuring that you do your best work on the day.

Get there calmly, get there early Leave home in plenty of time. You don't want to fall prey to traffic or transport situations, then arrive red-faced, panting and sweating like a racehorse. It gives the wrong impression, even if it's not your fault that you are off-schedule. Get a map so that you know exactly where you are going. Most schools have maps on their website; some will send you one with their audition info.

Drama schools are really hot on time-management and punctuality in their day-to-day running. So get smart and be cool, calm and collected as you stroll in a good fifteen minutes before the start time. You'll then have plenty of time to use the loo the four or five times that you will be needing, and also maybe to get a cup of tea and a Kit Kat. (Other chocolate-biscuit-type snacks are available.)

When you turn up, you will usually be met by staff and/or students. They are all there to help you, guide you and relax you. They want you to do well and will be trying (but not spying) to get an impression of you as a person.

Stay chilled Stay calm while you gently distill and refine what you want from this encounter. Don't get all hyped-up and panic-ridden. Feel and enjoy the flow of your adrenaline, but chill, too. You could even feel a tinge of excitement. This is your day!

Hangin' around – don't buy in to other people's negative energy There will, at times, be many nervous people. Don't buy in to their fear! Be nice and sociable but keep some personal space, so that you can concentrate calmly on the job.

Many of the nervous will, for sure, feel the need to talk too much. In situations such as these, people are apt to babble. They want to dissipate their tension and anxiety by spreading them into the ether or projecting them onto you. These people will want to tell you how nervous they are, or grill you on the pieces you are doing, etc., etc. They must not come between you and your purpose. Engage. Say 'hi', be nice, but get away if you have to, should it all become too much. Go to the toilet. Sneak outside for a second. Get some air. Sometimes earphones are brilliant; just don't actually attach them to an MP3 player.

Other nervous types like to be in your face with false confidence. Some may be saying they have just had a recall for RADA, LAMDA – ASDA… whatever! Good for them. Be pleased for them but don't let it affect your thinking, even if they are going in just before you. Forget about them; just make your immediate conditions work for you. Similarly, a candidate may come out of the audition room and blurt something similar to any of the following:

'Oh no, that was terrible.'

'I really messed that up, they didn't laugh once.'

'That was brilliant.'

'God, they are in such a bad mood.' [Rarely true.]

'They were really awful to me.' [Usually in his/her head only.]

'They were lovely.'

'That went really well.'

'That was really scary.'

Well, of course it's going to be scary. Scary is good. Scary is the buzz. Scary is why they invented bungee jumping! That's why people do acting. Sure, be neighbourly with people; just disengage when you need to. You may well bump into some overexcited, garrulous types who just want to talk about themselves. You haven't come to chat or make friends today; you've come to do your best work. And for that you need space and focus. If you really get on with someone, meet them for a coffee after.

Don't judge anything, or anybody – even you Being judgemental is not positive and is a waste of your time and serenity. Apply this to meeting people and also to any work that you do or witness.

Be generous to people you meet. Don't judge or think negatively of anyone, because you may end up having to partner them. It's much better to look for the good in everything and everyone on your audition day. If someone's a wally, love them for it. Always keep a good vibe.

Be you, be true The best impression you can give of yourself is an honest one. Be you, be true; it's all you can do.

Don't get all rushed If, when you get there, they ask if you want to go in early, if possible say: 'No thanks.' Say that you need the loo, or could do with a couple of seconds to compose yourself. Make things work for you.

Make this your time When they call you in, *know* that this is your time now. The auditioners are there for you. You have paid for the audition; you have travelled; you have worked, you have sweated.

Make sure you seize the day. Don't enter the room unfocused and too scared to marshal your goals and targets. Never leave the room thinking, 'Oh God, I was this', or 'I didn't achieve that.' You have to make it all count. To do that you must ignore everything else. Simply be in the moment when it counts.

So:

- **Make fear your friend – again.**
- **Wake up early, be positive – banish panic.**
- **Do your mantras: sort out what you want to achieve.**
- **Eat food.**
- **Get there early.**
- **Stay chilled. Keep a cool focus.**
- **Don't buy in to other people's negative energy.**
- **Don't judge.**
- **Be you, be true.**
- **Don't get all rushed.**
- **Make this your time.**

'Remember, it's so much better to be there early than be running to get there on time. You will be stressed enough, so you want to make sure you take away all other stressors — like being late! This also leaves you time to go over your pieces and get into the right mindset for your audition. You want to give yourself the best chance you can to do well. Also, do not underestimate how draining even a ten-minute audition will be and you need to keep on concentrating.' Fran

Just before you go in

Ask yourself: 'Am I truly ready for this?' And find that: 'Yes, I am!' Because:

- You are tranquil, yet charged.

- You have prepped methodically and with a journey.

- You have done your homework about the school.

- You are going to start well and end well.

- You know that you are not going to judge the panel or worry about them judging you.

- You also know that you are not going to fall victim to any bad habits when you perform and that you are going to be 'you' at all times.

- You are going to stay connected to every word, energised to the end of every thought.

- You are going to introduce change and not get trapped in one tone.

Remind yourself that you only get one shot Nothing must divert you from your purpose. Make the notion that you only get one shot something to spur your intent, not to scare you.

Don't let your status 'dwindle' 'Dwindling' is something people do when they meet others who seem to be in a position of power, or who can offer something they really want. The urge to fawn, crawl or giggle can be hard to resist. Match your status so that you encounter everyone as an equal. *Be prepared to have fun.* This is an exchange, an equal transaction. All of the staff on the panel would like to meet nice people and see their best work. You want the same sort of things, therefore you're equals. Only don't push your status too far the other way, and become swaggeringly confident.

In the Room:
Individual Auditions

What to do and how to be

Walk in well, but normally One of the hardest things in the world is to walk into a room full of strangers and say 'hello', however confident you are. Try to compose yourself and centre on being natural – nervous if you are, but neither nuts nor withdrawn.

Own the room – feel okay in the space When you get into the performance space, look around; get the feel of it. The room may be huge, it may be tiny – it doesn't matter. Whatever size or shape it may be, just be ready for it. Don't be intimidated by the room or what's in it: it's merely the space that will allow you to do – yep – your best work.

Don't try to figure out the panel – it doesn't matter The panel may be friendly (and usually they are), or indifferent, or tired, or quiet, or jolly. It doesn't matter.

Often, panel members don't look up much if they are listening and writing. They may be writing good things; they may be making less positive comments. What does this matter to you? They may laugh, they may not. *It doesn't matter.* Go with whatever happens. It's all good and nothing bad while you are in there, especially when you're performing. Let nothing put you off.

They may talk with you before or after your speeches – *it doesn't matter*. There may be no talking. This, too, means nothing. I have known people get recalls who simply went in, did their stuff and left – nothing more. Others get the full interview, directed, joked with and even shouted at. *It doesn't matter.* Just go with whatever happens.

Largely, they will be concentrating, and listening. So it may seem as if they don't like you, or are indifferent. This is hardly ever the case. All their attention is on you and what you are doing, and they would love to see you do it well. I can tell you that it is positively uplifting when someone who is cool, calm and collected *eventually* walks in, then sets their focus and connects up, then does a speech that engages and absorbs.

It's worth remembering that you could be asked: 'What you are going to perform today?' If you haven't already addressed this task, try it now. Go on. Just try it without tripping up or saying 'er' and 'um' more than four times. Make sure you don't get all 'formal'.

Get the distance right I nearly always have to ask people to stand back, so that I am not 'cluttered' by the performer's energies and have space to observe and write. Don't be too far away, though. Around six to nine good paces is about right, but it will depend on room size and where the panel is. Occasionally you will be asked to stand a long way off. But you will be okay with this because you have tried your speeches out at different distances from the audience.

Get your performance positions right If your piece is to another person, fix a mark somewhere in the room to anchor your eye level. Most schools *don't* want you to address the piece directly to the panel. (Though some, such as Guildhall, might ask for this.) If they don't want direct address, then *always* place the person you are talking to very slightly to the left or right of the panel – up to a metre is fine. **(X)** = the other character. The other character can be anywhere along the line between you and **(X)**.

VERY GOOD

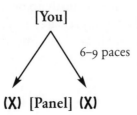

[You]

6–9 paces

(X) [Panel] **(X)**

Keep the character being addressed close to the panel, don't set the character too far to the left or right, as in the position below.

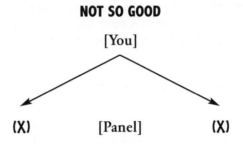

NOT SO GOOD

[You]

(X)   [Panel]   (X)

Don't put the character diametrically to your left or right (see below), otherwise all the panel will see is the side of your face, which can become irritating.

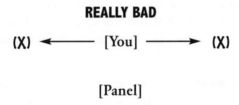

REALLY BAD

(X) ◄─────── [You] ───────► (X)

[Panel]

If you're doing two speeches, both involving another character, there is a slight advantage to be had from placing the second person on the opposite side for that speech.

Spin-starts? No Don't do them. Take a reasonable time to wire everything up. Just to refresh your memory, a 'spin-start' is when you spring the speech upon the panel as soon as you hear 'go'. If you do this, you will not be ready to do your best and neither will the panel be ready to appreciate it. You will even repel them slightly, rather than inviting them into the world you're creating. Therefore...

Start well I have broached 'start well' from several angles already, because this is so, so, *so* important. The panel usually says: 'When you're ready', or: 'In your own time.' They mean it. Take your time to create the moment and the world. But don't take all day, or do the 'now I am preparing to perform' show. So many people just launch into 'acting' without ever connecting to what they're doing.

- Set your mind and ambition to do your best work and recognise the fact that this *is* your one shot and that shot is *now*.

- Concentrate on what you want to do and what you don't want to do.

- Create the world and character. Who are you? Where are you? What's it all look like? Where is stuff?

- Inhabit the moment.

- Let the others in the room connect to you and your character's world, as you yourself start to connect to everything.

- Then – go!

Give your character a reason or an impetus to start speaking! Hear, in your head, the lines that have just been said to your character. These are the words that may well be prompting your character to react, to *decide* to speak. If not, run through what has just happened to you and why it happened. This will propel you into why you are speaking and what the *character* wants. The panel will be able to enter this world with you – and that also is exactly what *you* want.

The panel people will see your energy and persona change as you 'hear' and engage with what is being said. Then, you are not *merely* starting a 'speech'; you are the character, in the moment, speaking because you have to. You're speaking because you need something. Don't just launch into 'acting'.

If you didn't start well – *start again*! It's my belief that if you are not happy with what you are doing, and you're not too far along, you should just stop and say: 'I'm going to start again.' This might seem like an impossibly brave thing to do, but this is your moment. So stop and make sure they get your *finest* moment. Do it. You can. There's nothing to lose. Even if you are well along the way and feel you are not hitting it, change things!

There is no rule in any book ever written which says you have to stay on an unsatisfactory track, just because you started like that. You can change things in the next word. Grab hold of things and fix them! Don't just carry on thinking, 'Oh well, that was bad, so now I have to live with the rest of it being bad. Oh God, I'm so depressed, I'll just push on in the same rubbish vein... Okay where's my coat?'

Anyway, if you have another speech to do, you want it to be all good and not bad when you start it. In other words, always put yourself in a position to maximise your chances. Never leave the room feeling that you stopped yourself from doing your best work. Otherwise the whole exercise is pointless.

End well – Part 2 A lot of folk end really badly, without style or conviction. They disengage from the world of the character way too soon after the last line. This gives the impression that they have not engaged at all.

Stay with the end moment, and let the glow of what you have been doing settle. Stay in it and be proud. Don't step away with any kind of sheepish, self-destructive look. Don't apologise verbally, or with a self-effacing countenance. Even if you think you were rubbish, even if you were a complete git, the panel may well have seen something of interest. You never know. In all probability, you will be your worst critic. Let them be the judge of all that. Free yourself from that burden. End with a bang and not with a whimper. You owe it to yourself.

If it wasn't great (truly), then okay, fine. But onwards! You have another speech to redeem yourself with. Leave whatever demons, thoughts and judgements you may have, behind you.

Stay with it for the next speech If you have another one to do, remain in the zone and prepare yourself. Begin the second piece when you're ready; think only of doing your best work in this next effort. Assume nothing about what you have just done. Think nothing good or bad. Ruminate later, on the bus.

Going blank If you go blank or forget your lines – it doesn't matter! If what you have on offer is fresh, interesting and connected, this will not matter a jot. It's not a memory test. However, there are several courses of action:

- If it's early in the delivery, you can stop, gather yourself and start again.

- You can stop, stay in the moment, gather yourself and carry on.

- The one and only thing you *cannot* do is panic and break down.

Keep it together. Even professionals have moments when things screw up. Plenty of people who fluff lines, dry or worse, are recalled and even get in. It is about you, your potential and how you conduct yourself! Even if someone bursts into the room in the middle of your piece, just keep your composure. If you have embraced the mantras, you can handle anything now.

What if they want to direct me, or work with what I have done?
They may want to work with you on your speeches. They may not. If they don't – it doesn't matter. Do not fret. If they do – do not panic. Just listen, understand, and then go for what they are asking for with everything you've got. It's much better to come out of the speech and say, 'I think I may have overdone that a bit, I can tone it down if you like,' than to know you didn't hit what they were asking for and did nothing to rectify that. This is your moment.

Audition audits:

- Walk in well, but normally.

- It's all about making clean, true connections with the people you meet at the audition and with your work.

- Don't try to figure out the panel.

- Get the distance right.

- Get your performance positions right.

- Don't do spin-starts.

- Start well.

- Give your character a reason or an impetus to start speaking.

- If you didn't start well – start again.

- End well.

- Stay with it for the next speech.

- Glitches, hiccups, cock-ups: if you don't show it, they won't know it. You get points for composure.

- Go for it if they want to work with you. Don't worry or wonder.

After the Audition

After each audition, take stock of what happened. Did the auditioners work with you? Scribble down what they asked. Note any comments they may have made regarding your choices or delivery. These are golden nuggets for future encounters, particularly if they recall you.

Was there anything you could have said or done better? Make a note. Meditate, then act upon your experience. Over the years I have given out feedback forms to students to fill in, post-audition (there are many of these on this book's website, www.excellentauditions.co.uk). It helps them to assimilate the experience.

Note

The audition panel may have worked with you in a specific way, which doesn't mean that what you offered was wrong or bad, rather that they were looking for change and flexibility. Also, each tutor you work with has her or his own taste, so remember this at the next audition. Different schools will take differing angles, so you could get conflicting comments. No need to get confused. It's just a case of taking it all on board, then finding your own path through.

Between Auditions

It's all good and nothing bad, no matter what is happening for you – recalls or not. Just keep working on your head and your acting. Take note of your faults, or things that didn't go so well, and fix them. Keep going. Never give in!

There are no apparent rules as to who gets in and who doesn't, apart from the obvious qualities of potential talent, trainability and amenability. Every year I see a couple of people fail to make it who I would have bet my shirt on to get in. I also see totally unexpected cases get snapped up. I have known quite a few people who didn't get even a wink from the panel for most of their auditions. Then eventually – sometimes even on their last audition – recall, recall, boom… *in*! You just can't tell. So everything is up for grabs right till the end. Never give in.

All you can do is keep maximising your chances by staying strong and positive. *It's not over till it's over.* Keep learning, keep working, even if you have to go right back to the start, back to basics. Those who fight on will do better. The fight will, at this stage, be largely in your head, with your self-esteem and your stamina.

Celebrate the success of those around you if they are getting the odd result. Positive!

If you are getting a few rejections, it's always good policy to reassess your speeches. Maybe they don't work as well for you now? If you have a few extra pieces ready to roll, you won't have to scramble around for a new one.

Recall Stages

Generally, these will be physically and mentally demanding, stretching and exacting, but also humane and light-hearted. They are led by highly talented, professional and caring teaching staff and are usually enjoyable. Get into the whole physical and mental challenge. If you have fun, you'll have a positive and potentially more successful experience. The tutors and directors with whom you'll be working will be interested in you 'the person', as well as you 'the actor'. This stage of your audition is all about interaction.

Read the details of what they send you Be very sure you have read every letter – to the letter. Know what they want you to prepare.

What happens at a recall? All places are slightly different and change their requirements subtly from year to year. Some do the whole thing – first audition to recalls – in a day. Others, like RADA, will call you back to an encounter similar to the first one before recalling you several more times.

You might get an offer to attend an all-day or even two-day workshop. These are group events. They will consist of intensive classes, usually covering movement, voice, and group improvisation/devising. Go for it, even if they ask crazy things of you. Look for creativity and spontaneity. Basically, are you up for anything? You'll also get to sing, if you haven't already done so, and do further monologue work. Your back-up speech could well get called into play now. (See 'Group auditions'.)

A few schools are currently into sight-reading – sometimes from Dickens and Carroll, where the descriptions are rich and the characters are boldly drawn. Don't worry about sight-reading, they just want to see how you lift language from the page. Also, don't worry if you are a tad dyslexic. You will have told them in your application. You could just remind them, though.

THE AUDITIONS

Usually there will be more interviews, and they can be much more rigorous than before. You might feel some pressure during these. Relax, and roll with it.

Panels may well be larger in number and the people you see might be different this time around. Current students will often be present for you to work with. Go with what the students offer. Don't be thrown. *Use* the people they give you. This is to test your focus and your ability to interact with someone else, whilst in the moment. Trust the moment, trust them and trust your instincts.

Try to do your speeches with, and to, another person in your recall prep. Make the other person be interactive.

Renew your will. You aren't home yet. Renew your energies If you nail a recall, well done! But you're nowhere near home yet. It will be very easy at this stage to go off the boil. You may by now feel less worried, a bit more experienced, slightly smug at your success and quite cool. This is the time for the real hard effort!

You are so close but you could be so far off. This is still a test of your will, of how much you want it, and of your mental stamina. It is often at this point in the game that you can get weary or, even worse, complacent. Hey, why not? They like you. You're hot; you got through; thousands didn't. Just remember, all the others who did the same are also hot: that's why they got through. They are now in direct competition with you. But don't let that scare you, because they are not you and, anyway, you are just here to do your best work!

Now is the time to refocus. Renew your energy and make sure you don't blow it, now you are this near. Look back to the stuff about group auditions, because many of your recalls will be group events.

Do not get complacent Many people have fallen at this stage through want of a bit of willpower and effort. It is a fact that the better you do in your auditions, the longer the whole campaign will last and the wearier you will become. Many schools have multiple recalls, so if you're getting these you could still be at it in June.

The longer all this takes, the less willing everyone is to look at their pieces in rehearsal. If you fall into this mindset, you will go stale and your work will lose its edge. I have seen this so many times.

Scary thoughts You are, possibly, going to be a bit scared to work on your stuff because, *secretly*, you are worried that you have indeed lost your edge. This will be scary, as will the notion that you have to go back to basics and strip it all back and start again. Yes, at this stage it *is* a scary thought, and something you won't want to do... But if you don't stay on top of things and it all drifts into a soupy, soggy, sloppy mess, then you won't make it.

I can't count the number of times, at this crucial juncture, that I've had candidates say to me that they are okay; they feel good about things and they want to keep the pieces fresh by not over-doing them – only to see, when they do, eventually, show their speeches, rubbish and degenerated work. This reluctance is understandable. After so long and so much work, it becomes almost painful to dig deep and scrutinise your own work. *But you must shake off this mindset.*

Work with them The panel will want to work on your pieces. In these situations, go for it; don't wonder or guess. Work *with* them on the speeches they request. It's all about how you work and interact with them. You would be doing this with them for three years. They want to be sure that they can sustain this with you – for three years.

Get fit – build stamina As I have said, some classes are very demanding. Some are military-style workouts. People return from a day or weekend of recalls totally whacked. Make sure you are building your stamina for your campaign.

Recalled points:

- Read, understand and act upon the info the schools will send you.

- Renew your will.

- Don't get complacent.

- Keep your speeches fresh by working them.

- Work with the tutors. Go for it.

- Get fit.

On Recall Days

Get excited Rather than mooch about 'like foggy south, puffing with wind and rain' and letting this occasion daunt you (which you won't, because fear is now your friend), look upon this as a chance to work, in depth for a day or two – with the best. How exciting! How cool is that? You get to work with them on *you* and your acting. What an amazing experience, whether you get in or not. People usually have to pay big money for this.

Be ready and up for anything As I've said, the one certainty from now on is that the school is really going to test you. It may even feel at times that people are trying to break you. They aren't, but they do want to see what you are made of.

The tutors might want to know if you can take criticism. So be prepared to do crazy things and to withstand provocative questions, comments and direction. Take it all seriously, but enjoy, have fun! Stay positive and flexible. If you are still quite young, they will be seeking to gauge your maturity. You'll just have to prove your mature mettle and convince them that you are ready for drama-school training.

I've heard plenty of people come back saying, 'OMG, they really, really, *really* hated me and everything I did.' And then be offered a place. You just have to stay brave, open-minded, good-humoured and positive, even under what may feel like withering crossfire. It's all good and nothing bad.

All about the work – no wondering Don't try to impress, don't wonder if you are being impressive. Listen and understand. Make it all about the work; don't make it about you being good or wondering if you are being good or getting it right. Don't waste energy or focus wondering about the other candidates, either. Like I said – it's all about working *with* them.

Long days – stay on duty! This is really, really important! These are long and tough days. Many auditionees lose their focus and concentration at various stages in the day because of the intensity of it all. With physical fatigue comes mental tiredness. Really be on guard against switching off. Never go off-duty! Say to yourself at points through the day 'Refresh!' or 'Renew your energy!' Sounds a bit hippy, but it works.

Group work, again Be a team player. It's always good to remind yourself of what's what. The school is looking to build a team; a company who are going to cooperate creatively and imaginatively, with generosity and sensitivity towards the efforts of others. Take your moments when they come, of course, but then be sure to support the work of others. The panel will be seriously testing your ability to operate in a group and also how you act, react and interact with fellow performers. Once again, support the work in the room. If you don't or can't do some of the exercises, don't panic, stay positive, it won't be the end of the world. It's about your spirit.

Younger recalled people If you are in your teens, you may feel pressed somewhat in interview and exercises. Stay cool, smile. Cope.

After the Auditions

When it's all over, if you made it – good for you. If you didn't, you may have some thinking to do. You may also be a bit down, feeling rejected and talentless. This is good. Feel these things. Accept them. Then stop. Take a holiday, get a job, earn some cash, meet people and then think about whether or not you want to go through the whole thing again. This process, both head and heart, is what acting is all about.

If the itch, the burn is still there, then have another short break and then turn back to the front of this book and I will be with you every step of the way.

End well...

Well, that's about all I have to say. It was written from the heart, with all best wishes and a sincere will for you to get where you need to be. Of course, there is a load more, but hey, they'll tell you all about that at drama school...

In the meantime, keep working, stay positive and keep the mantras with you. All good, nothing bad... All good, nothing bad... All good.

Here are some last words from someone who made it. Firstly, just before going to drama school:

'This was me when I found out: "What?! Are you sure? Ahhhhhhhhhhhhhhhhh thank you soooo much." Yes yes yes f***ing YES!! Woohoo!'

And just after drama school:

'I was absolutely elated when I found out that I had a place on the Three-Year Acting Course at Guildhall, and auditions and working on pieces just melted into joy and anticipation. I did it! I was there! As scary as the prospect of auditioning may seem, it is more than worth it when your hard work pays off. My three years at Guildhall were the most challenging, awakening and character-building of my life so far. If you really want to embark upon this uncertain, scary but ultimately wonderful and fulfilling career, then I would say work hard for your auditions, stay focused and positive and keep a MASSIVE sense of humour and perspective!

Most importantly, don't make it all about getting a place. Be yourself in auditions, as that is what they want to see. It takes the pressure off a bit too, as that is all you can be!

:) I wish you all the luck in the world.' Dani

PS: *'So do I…'* AJ

Appendices

Likely Questions at Your Interview

If you take time to think about these questions, what lies behind them becomes much clearer. I will give some pointers as to what the panel might really be asking.

Be honest, but don't flood the place with negativity. Critical, objective awareness is the thing here. Think about what went well and the things that you might have hit a bit better. The keyword here is 'think'. As with any question, give yourself time to consider what is being asked, and then work out what you want to say.

'What have you been doing with yourself lately?'

'How do you think it went? [They mean your pieces.] How do you feel?'

These are popular and universal questions, but can be very tricky. It's really worth having a think about what you have been up to. This can include any jobs, travel, marathon-running, etc., as well as things theatrical. In your reply, be fluent and interesting but not rehearsed. Even if you think what you've been doing is really mundane, celebrate that.

'Who is your favourite actor/actress?'

They might mean stage not screen, so check with them. This question is harder to answer if it means stage acting, because it is not always easy to have seen the same person in different stage productions. But maybe it could be a performance that you have admired.

'Why do you want to come here?'

You should know why, and if you don't it could be seen as something of an insult that you know nothing about that particular institution and what it stands for. It's vital to address this point. If you've done your groundwork, managed to talk to current students at that particular place and seen some performances there, then you'll have no trouble with this line of questioning.

'What can we offer you?'

The answer to this is linked to the question above. It's about their school and what they do, as much as it is about you and your needs. Why are they important to your training and to your career as an actor?

Think about your needs and why you want to train. Also, what you want to learn and improve on. The type of environment you want to be in for the next three years. The kind of people you want to be with and work with, and the specific inspiration and challenges you're after.

Questions may be based on your CV, application form and personal statement. So keep a copy and read it just before you go.

'What can you offer us?'

Everyone hates this one, but be calm and be honest. If you think it through, it will come. What are they looking for, do you think, in a candidate? This question is about you, but if you could make it about you *and* them, that would be even better.

'Where do you see yourself in ten years' time?'

This question could be asking many things, but here are some possibilities. How do you see your career developing? While we all want to be successful, it's true that few of us would turn our noses up at some additional degree of fame and fortune. But realistically, the panel is also asking about your drive and ambition. Perhaps even the kind of work you'd like to be doing and with whom. For example, quality work that matters, on a regular basis, with inspiring people? Or perhaps just 'making a living'?

'What plays have you seen recently?'

Can you talk about them? It's very common to freeze and clam up on this topic. Just refresh your memory. Make notes as you see stuff.

'What is the function of the theatre?'

Gosh... er...

'What's the worst/best experience you've ever had?'

Be honest... A funny worst moment is always good for a laugh. Also, find out if they mean in life or on stage.

'What will you do if you don't get in?'

Think about determination, commitment and persistence.

'Do you think actors are always searching for something inside themselves?'

'What is the purpose of study and training?'

You are learning a craft. You are using your mind, creativity, emotions, intellect, voice and body. You will need to expand and strengthen these things. Study and training are the gateway to power and understanding that you could not otherwise possess.

'Have you read our prospectus?'

'Do you know anything about us? Have you done any research at all?'

'Tell me what the play is about.'

You'd better have read it and understood it, otherwise you might come across as the kind of corner-cutting, non-meticulous type that the school doesn't want.

'If you were directing this speech, what would you say to the actor?'

'Do you know what you are doing and why you have made certain choices?'

'Why did you choose this piece – and this character?'

Yes, why did you?

'How have you approached the character?'

Here they are looking for what kind of prep you have done, and what your thinking is on the character.

'What character decisions have you made?'

'What about the body language of the character?'

'When you started the speech, did you have a reason?'

This is about what your character wants. What prompts them to start speaking?

'Why did you choose these particular speeches?'

If you went through the right process to select your speeches, then you will know this automatically.

'Describe yourself in four words.'

Don't baulk. They want you to react. Be spontaneous or think about it – it's your answer, but don't be resistant.

'What colour would you associate yourself with?'

See above.

'What's on at your local theatre? Who's in it? Who is the director? Who is the designer?'

They probably won't ask you this, but it will be impressive if you can drop in this sort of info, since it reveals both how interested you are in what's going on and your commitment to watching other people's work.

'Is there any actor you'd like to be?'

'What was the last part you did?'

'Why do you want to go to drama school?'

Know why? Check your personal statement!

'What do you want from training?'

'Do you consider yourself crazy to want to be an actor?'

What are they asking?

'What interests you about Shakespeare?'

'Which Shakespearean character would you most like to play?'

'If Hamlet were an MP today, who would he be?'

'Do you think acting is important?'

Do you? Why? No clichés.

'Where else have you applied?'

This is not a trick question: tell them.

'How did you get on?' [At the previous places]

Be honest but as positive as possible. If something at a previous audition was a nightmare, celebrate it and present it in a positive light: 'It was a nightmare; I was such an idiot…'

'Why do you want to be an actor?'

You should know this. Again, no clichés, please. Is it just to be on stage, to be famous?

'Are you a disciplined worker?'

- **Listen and understand.**
- **Be eloquent not garrulous. Think first.**
- **Be alert not fidgety.**
- **Be open not closed.**
- **Be generous not mean.**
- **Say what you mean.**
- **Mean what you say.**

Some Suitable Audition Songs

They are pretty much all from musical shows, because these give a good range and depth of play. Don't rule out non-show tunes, but beware of shallow, 'poppy' numbers that might be harder to connect with and leave you with little room to show breadth and range in your delivery. Rock'n'roll-era ballads can be really good too.

These below are all good for throwing your energy and charm into. They can be spoken/sung in places, which might help with some of the tough notes.

Soprano:

'I Could Have Danced All Night' from *My Fair Lady*
'Vanilla Ice Cream' from *She Loves Me*
'Wishing You Were Somehow Here Again' / 'Think of Me' from
    The Phantom of the Opera
'I Have Confidence' / 'Climb Ev'ry Mountain' from *The Sound of*
    Music
'I Don't Know How to Love Him' from *Jesus Christ Superstar*
'Unexpected Song' from *Song and Dance*
'Another Suitcase in Another Hall' from *Evita*
'What I Did for Love' from *A Chorus Line*
'Astonishing' from *Little Women*
'Baby Mine' from Disney's *Dumbo*
'If I Were a Bell' from *Guys and Dolls*
'Mr. Snow' / 'You'll Never Walk Alone' from *Carousel*

'I Feel Pretty' from *West Side Story*
'Someone to Watch Over Me' from *Porgy and Bess*
'Ribbons Down my Back' from *Hello, Dolly!*
'My Funny Valentine' / 'Where or When' from *Babes in Arms*
'So in Love' from *Kiss Me, Kate*
'Jimmy' from *Thoroughly Modern Millie*

Mezzo/Alto:

'Candle on the Water' from Disney's *Pete's Dragon*
'My Favourite Things' from *The Sound of Music*
'Better' / 'Here Alone' / 'Days of Plenty' from *Little Women*
'Heaven Help my Heart' / 'Someone Else's Story' from *Chess*
'The Colors of My Life' from *Barnum*
'There's a Fine, Fine Line' from *Avenue Q*
'As Long as He Needs Me' from *Oliver!*
'I'm Not That Girl' from *Wicked*
'Still Hurting' from *The Last Five Years*
'Suddenly It Happens' / Tell Him Anything (But Not That I Love Him) from *The Slipper and the Rose*
'You Are My Lucky Star' from *Singin' in the Rain*
'In My Own Little Corner' from *Cinderella*
'Hold On' from *The Secret Garden*
'Adelaide's Lament' from *Guys and Dolls*
'Bill' from *Show Boat*
'Secret Love' from *Calamity Jane*
'Pulled' from *The Addams Family*
'Home' from *The Wiz*
'Get Out and Stay Out' from *9 to 5*

Tenor:

'Breeze Off the River' from *The Full Monty*
'Winter's on the Wing' from *The Secret Garden*
'Take a Chance on Me' / 'Small Umbrella in the Rain' from *Little Women*

'Go the Distance' from Disney's *Hercules*
'Lost in the Wilderness' from *Children of Eden*
'Corner of the Sky' from *Pippin*
'If I Loved You' from *Carousel*
'Luck Be a Lady' from *Guys and Dolls*
'Why God Why?' from *Miss Saigon*
'Younger Than Springtime' from *South Pacific*
'All I Need is the Girl' from *Gypsy*
'Bring Him Home' from *Les Misérables*
'This is the Moment' from *Jekyll & Hyde*
'I'm Alive' from *Next to Normal*
'Pilate's Dream' from *Jesus Christ Superstar*
'Maria' / 'Tonight' / 'Something's Coming' from *West Side Story*
'Different' from *Honk!*
'Hushaby Mountain' from *Chitty Chitty Bang Bang*
'Giants in the Sky' from *Into the Woods*
'Love Changes Everything' from *Aspects of Love*

Baritone:

'Anthem' from *Chess*
'Being Alive' from *Company*
'Some Enchanted Evening' from *South Pacific*
'Who I'd Be' from *Shrek the Musical*
'Pure Imagination' from *Willy Wonka & the Chocolate Factory*
'Fortune Favors the Brave' from *Aida*
'Pinball Wizard' from *Tommy*
'One Song Glory' from *RENT*
'The Impossible Dream' from *Man of La Mancha*
'Leaning on a Lamppost' from *Me and My Girl*
'If I Can't Love Her' from *Beauty and the Beast*
'Edelweiss' from *The Sound of Music*
'Something was Missing' from *Annie*
'Be Prepared' from Disney's *The Lion King*
'My Name' from *Oliver!*

Other Acting Books from Nick Hern Books

The Acting Book
John Abbott

Actions: The Actor's Thesaurus
Marina Caldarone and Maggie Lloyd-Williams

Becoming an Actor
Thomasina Unsworth

The Golden Rules of Acting
Andy Nyman

So You Want To Be An Actor?
Timothy West and Prunella Scales

So You Want To Be In Musicals?
Ruthie Henshall and Daniel Bowling

So You Want To Work In Theatre?
Susan Elkin

So You Want To Go To Drama School?
Helen Freeman

Monologue Books from Nick Hern Books

Classical Monologues
edited by Marina Caldarone

Contemporary Monologues
edited by Trilby James

Shakespeare Monologues
edited by Luke Dixon

Shakespeare Monologues for Young People
edited by Luke Dixon

Each title is available for male and female actors and contains at least forty excellent audition speeches.

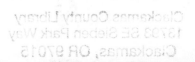

www.nickhernbooks.co.uk

facebook.com/nickhernbooks

twitter.com/nickhernbooks